FOOTPLATE DAYS ON THE SOUTHERN

FOOTPLATE DAYS ON THE SOUTHERN

H. NORMAN

BRADFORD BARTON

ISBN 0 85153 451 1

Produced by Lovell Baines Print Ltd for the publishers

D. BRADFORD BARTON LTD *Trethellan House · Truro · Cornwall*

384L4

CONTENTS

CHAPTER ONE

Early days, and a false start

I was not interested in railways. Well not to start with. I grew up during the Second World War, evacuated from London to the West Country, and my abiding interest then – and one that remains with me – was aviation. At the end of the war I returned home, and the new school that I attended was situated a few yards from the Southern Railway main line from Victoria to the Kent Coast. Immediately after the war there was an upsurge in interest in railways due to the production of the well known ABC booklets of Ian Allan which, as never before, gave a complete numerical list of the locomotives of each of the railway companies, and started the vogue of loco-spotting.

Soon most of my fellows possessed one of these little books and were diligently underlining those locomotives they had 'copped'. Alas, I must admit to one trait in my character which can sometimes be an asset, sometimes not. I am sure that my best friends and those that are not would certainly agree that at times I can be a trifle stubborn. So it was with what I considered the latest craze; I was not going to join in so trivial an occupation and, indeed, for a long time I took no part in it.

One of the problems for the teachers was that the main line ran very close to the school and at times pupils would sneak glances out of the windows at the passing trains when their minds should have been on scholastic matters, so much so that to counter the distraction of the railway some of the classrooms had the lower windows whitewashed to obliterate the view! This I think aroused my interest, possibly it could be a triumph getting the numbers despite the efforts being made to prevent us doing so, and also I had noticed one thing that made me curious. Every day two particular tank engines would pass the school at high speed running light i.e. without a train, whether they were going towards London or away from it. The engines concerned were 1706 and 1710. Many years later I learned that they ran daily to and from Stewarts Lane to Farningham Road to work the branch line from that station to Gravesend West. The upshot was that I bought an ABC of Southern Railway locomotives and started spotting.

Initially I was satisfied with recording those engines that passed the school but soon I joined some of my friends when they journeyed to Nine Elms and Stewarts Lane locomotive sheds and was amazed by the number and variety of engines to be seen.

Another attraction of such visits was the excitement of sneaking past the foreman's office, in which we were not always successful. They were men who were capable of striking terror in our hearts, as well as ejecting us from the premises in none too friendly a fashion.

At Nine Elms, as well as the Merchant Navy class (most of which were still in wartime black, although a few of the last of the first twenty which were then brand-new were appearing in malachite green) there was a fascinating variety of pre-grouping locomotives of London & South Western origin. They comprised 0-4-4 tank engines of the M7 and 02 classes; 4-4-0 tender engines of the K10, L11, and T9 classes; 4-6-0 tender engines of the H15 class; plus the old rebuilt Drummond 4-6-0 of the T14 class, with their huge eight-wheel water-cart tenders, which weighed over 50 tons when fully coaled. In addition to these, there were three distinct oddities in the shape of two of Stroudley's D1 tank engines, 2286 and 2289, which were in permanent store. I only saw one of them in steam once, in the height of summer, acting as the coal hopper pilot. The other odd man out was the shed shunting locomotive, which never left the shed, but pottered around moving lines of locomotives from one road to another, an old 0-8-0 tank engine that the Southern had obtained from the Kent & East Sussex Railway in 1932 named *Hecate*. In attendance as well were the King Arthur, Lord Nelson, and S15 classes of the Southern Railway, as well as the Remembrance class 4-6-0s.

At Stewarts Lane all the engines were pre-war in origin, the most modern being the King Arthur and Schools classes plus the Maunsell moguls, with a large number of ex-South Eastern & Chatham engines of much older vintage.

To go from school to the sheds involved travelling one stop on the South London line, which at that time was worked by the original L.B.S.C.R. alternating current trains, which had been converted to direct current, and reduced from three to two car sets by the Southern Railway. They were built in 1909, solid vehicles of slab-sided appearance, which gave a magnificently smooth ride, mounted as they were on girder-type underframes. The bogies gave out a distinct rattle and as a result we nick-named them 'buckets', due to the similarity to the rattle of a bucket handle. These old soldiers worked on until the mid-1950s when they were scrapped; in view of their unique history surely one should have been preserved?

In addition to Southern Railway trains, others from both the L.M.S. and L.N.E.R. passed the school. The L.M.S. ones were goods, principally from Cricklewood to Hither Green, usually hauled by the original Jinty tanks built by the Midland Railway, numbered 7200 upwards, or very occasionally a 4F, or parcels trains hauled by Fowler 2-6-2 tank engines. The L.N.E.R. goods trains were hauled by either the N1 or J52 classes of tank engines of G.N.R. origin, with just now and then a train from the Great Eastern section being hauled by a J15, or perhaps one of the big ex-G.E.R. six-coupled tender engines.

As time went by, I had visited all the Southern haunts around the London area and in mid-1946 managed to afford a visit to the Mecca of the Southern, Eastleigh. Apart from the usual engines, there were a number of rare ones. I still have some details of that visit; the last Adams 4-4-0 express engine in service (658), paintwork and copper burnished to perfection, indicating the pride which the staff took in her, in contrast to her sister engine, 657. This was in dirty pre-war condition, with the large numbers on the tender, standing on the scrap road in the depot, having served her time as a hot water engine for the Merchant Navy class at Exmouth Junction. Possibly her greatest moments, however, had been some ten years earlier when she had been the express engine in Will Hays film "Oh! Mr. Porter".

With 657 on the scrap road were dozens of old Adams A12 0-4-2 tender engines awaiting their turn to be dismembered in the works, as well as Brighton Atlantic 2040 *St. Catherine's Point* minus tender, which had been withdrawn from service in January 1944. If this might be thought to have been a long time awaiting breaking up, much older engines were on the lines outside the works, for the Southern fortunately was never in any hurry to dispose of its withdrawn stock. Still awaiting extinction 13 years after being withdrawn was the old Beattie saddle tank 0334, painted grey. True it was without its boiler, looking somewhat unusual with its saddle tank sitting on top of the frames, and it was to wait another three years before being cut up. Behind it were two Isle of Wight engines, Brighton Terriers W10 and W12, still in the old green paint they had run in years before. They had not turned a revenue earning wheel for years and were destined never to do so again. Returned from the Island in May 1936, they remained at Eastleigh until broken up in March 1949. On another road were three Stroudley D1 0-4-2 tanks; 2627, painted green, a resident since 1943; 2232, arrived 1944; and one that had only just taken root, 2240.

So time went by, at length my sixteenth birthday arrived, and the question of a career arose. My educational accomplishments were adequate, without the embarassment of being outstanding, and I quite frankly had no idea of what I wanted to do. Eventually, after considering a number of possibilities, my thoughts turned to a railway career – but as what? After much deliberation I decided that perhaps there might be a worthwhile future in qualifying as an engineer and accordingly I wrote to the Southern and London & North Eastern Railways enquiries as to the possibilities. I was offered by both the chance of a premium apprenticeship at a cost of £50 or an ordinary apprenticeship. With the Southern this would mean moving to Ashford or Brighton which I was not keen to do, whilst the L.N.E.R. offered Doncaster, or Stratford in East London. This latter situation attracted me and so I accepted the offer of an ordinary apprenticeship, £50 being a vast sum of money in 1948.

At five o'clock on the morning of 5th January 1948 I was startled out of my sleep by the alarm clock. This was the first shock of working for a living, getting up at an hour I never knew existed until now. I started at Stratford at seven and had nearly an hours journey via the Northern and newly extended Central Lines of the Underground before getting there. On arrival, I was briefly interviewed by a Mr. Brown who was undoubtedly the great factotum; this was clear because he wore that one time great symbol of authority on the railway, a bowler hat. I seem to recall, apart from being told of the importance of punctuality, and of doing everything I was told to do by anyone immediately (if not sooner), no reference to or outline of my future career, save that I was going to be an assistant to the storekeeper for a time. So I spent the next few weeks in the stores issuing tools and parts from the hundreds of items held. Inevitably I had requests for right-handed hammers or left-handed screwdrivers etc, until my tormenters tired of the sport or until I was wise enough to outwit them.

We had one hour for lunch and, after a while, I took much of this time having a look round the works and also the loco, which I believe at that time was the biggest in the country, for of course most of the suburban service from Liverpool Street was at that time still steam worked, in addition to the main line services. There were hoards of G.E.R. 2-4-2 and 0-6-2 tank engines in addition to 9000, the first of the Thompson L1 tanks, resplendent in apple green, for these commuter services, as well as the G.E.R. six coupled tank and tender engines.

Great Eastern B12 4-6-0s with inside cylinders abounded, in company with the Gresley B17s, plus D15 and D16 Claud Hamiltons for the main line trains, with a few B1s beginning to appear.

Like Eastleigh, Stratford, as well as repairing locomotives, scrapped them as well but had given up building them some years previously, and at this time there were long lines of F3 tank engines awaiting scrapping; and there were also the last engines of the former Midland & Great Northern Railway, J93 class tanks 8484 and 8488. Parts of these engines had by repute started life on the Cornwall Minerals Railway in 1874. One other interesting engine awaiting the same fate was the last 4-4-4 tank in Great Britain, the former Metropolitan Railway engine, L.N.E.R. No.7512.

The works itself was provided with a few locomotives to move engines and materials about, the most celebrated being those of the J92 class, which had cranes mounted on them. They were the oldest engines in service with any of the main line railways, having been built in 1868; instead of having running numbers they were lettered A to C. During the time that I was working in the stores a diminutive 0-4-0 coffee pot tank of class Y5 was used to shunt wagons in and out of the shops. This little engine was kept spotless by its crew. Imagine my surprise, therefore, two days after I had last seen it working, to see it distributed in so many pieces in two wagons being despatched to a scrap merchants.

A little while later, I was transferred to the Engine Repair Shop, which was away from the original buildings where I had been working, and situated more to the north of the loco shed. Here all the general repairs were carried out. My job was to operate a lathe, mostly finishing work on components such as machining wash-out plugs etc.

Whilst I was there, the first engine to complete its overhaul and be repainted in British Railways livery left the works, for the railways had been nationalised on 1st January 1948. This was J69 class 8619, which was painted in L.N.E.R. apple green and given the prefix E to its number, as well as the full legend BRITISH RAILWAYS in yellow at the top of the tanks. Certainly she presented a fine sight when wheeled out and specially posed for official photographs. She was used for many years as the Liverpool Street station pilot. My own little bit of personal railway history at this time was preparing wash-out plugs for the streamlined B17 *East Anglian*. There was considerable pride exhibited in their jobs by many of the shop's staff and several thought it something to be called upon to work on this particular engine. But I was none too happy. The repetitive work, poor conditions, and not knowing where I was going in the scheme of things, plus the poor pay of 21 shillings a week, did not give me a sense of vocation. After agonising for a week or two, I decided my venture into railway work was not the thing for me and yet I was still keen to contribute to the railway. How to achieve this was the question. What about a footplate life then? Surely this was the answer and moreover, I could perhaps get a job on the Southern, which would save my two-hour journey per day. My mind was made up. I wrote to the Southern.

CHAPTER TWO

A New Beginning

The reply was not long in coming. I opened the envelope with bated breath. I was asked to report to the shedmaster for an interview at Stewarts Lane on 9th March 1948. Forthwith I decided to burn my boats and accordingly terminated my employment with Eastern Region, saying goodbye to Stratford on the 5th March. No-one implored me to stay!

It was a novel experience presenting myself to the watchman at the entrance to the shed in Dickens Street, Battersea, armed with an official invitation. Hitherto, entrance had sometimes been unofficially gained at the less impregnable entrance off Corunna Terrace, providing one could sneak past the shed foreman's office when he was busy. The watchman gave me directions to reach the shedmaster's office.

This was the only time I met Mr. A.J. Winchester, who at that time was the shedmaster. I remember little now of the interview, except that I was anxious to impress as much as possible and, at the termination of the interview, he told me that I would be accepted as a cleaner at Stewarts Lane provided I passed the medical examination, which had to be taken at London Bridge station the following day. This duly took place in a remarkably dingy brown office. I recall that at the end of the examination nothing was said to me but I was given a sealed envelope addressed to the shedmaster at Stewarts Lane. I went back on the South London line and, as we ran into South Bermondsey station, saw in the distance an ex-Brighton K Class mogul waiting to run onto the main line from Bricklayers Arms loco. I hoped against hope that I would have the opportunity of working on the footplate of what must have been the handsomest design of that wheel arrangement, although in fact they were a rarity at Stewarts Lane. I was asked to wait until the letter was taken to the shedmaster and at length a clerk reappeared. "You can start work at six tomorrow morning", he told me – golden words indeed! I collected two sets of overalls from the stores and returned home with a light heart.

The 11th March 1948 was overcast and damp. Standing inside the depths of the shed, cold and dead, was "German" 1764 resplendent in Southern Railway green livery. I had been armed by the foreman cleaner with a plentiful supply of cotton waste and a can of "cream" oil which was reserved for green engines (for black engines paraffin was the order of the day). With the willing addition of elbow grease I set to work cleaning 1764 and a couple of hours later she shone like a new pin, whereas I resembled a coal scuttle – having in the process transferred much from my inanimate friend to my own person. One part of the job I distinctly did not like was having to climb inside the motions of the inside cylinder engines and clean the connecting rods, valve motion and all that went with it which, of course, due to the necessary lubrication, gathered a lot of dirt and in turn required a lot of cleaning in very cramped conditions.

As the days went by, I became much more closely associated with many of the engines that some six months earlier I had seen from a distance passing my old school and found certainly that looking at them was a sight cleaner and less exhausting occupation than working on them. I had as well to get used to shift working; starting at six was no trial to me, as I had always been an early riser but going to work at two o'clock in the afternoon was strange. Worst still was night work, starting at ten o'clock and, although I have done a lot of night work since then, I have never liked it.

It was surprising to note the large number of pre-Grouping engines still in service at Stewarts Lane, mostly of ex-South Eastern & Chatham Railway origin, as of course the shed was of London Chatham & Dover Railway origin, the amalgamation with the South Eastern taking place in 1899, which gave birth to the South Eastern & Chatham.

The oldest and strangest looking engine on the shed was also the only representative of the old South Eastern Railway there. This was 1302, the sole engine of the 1302 class, an 0-4-0 crane tank built long ago in 1881, with the (long inoperative) crane mounted on the chimney. 1302 was used about once every two weeks, when the regular pilot engine in the nearby C.W.S. milk depot was absent for a day having a boiler wash-out. The Westinghouse brake was another long defunct appendage on this veteran and braking was effected by proceeding at a very slow waddle (the engine in motion gave a very good imitation of a bird), with the fireman furiously winding on the handbrake, to come to a stop with the wooden brake blocks as soon as possible.

Slightly younger were the two representatives at that time of the old London Chatham & Dover Railway, T class 0-6-0 tank engines Nos. 1602 and 1604, which were in fact local lads, as they were built at Longhedge

Works in 1893 and 1891 respectively. I say at that time for, as I shall relate, we did somewhat later acquire another L.C.D.R. engine. Longhedge Works was that old L.C.D.R. locomotive works before the amalgamation of 1899 and was sited to the rear of the loco shed at Stewarts Lane. It ceased to produce locomotives in the early 1900s when construction was concentrated on Ashford but it was still functioning, giving intermediate and general overhauls to quite a number of engines every year. 1604 had spent its entire life working from Stewarts Lane, except for a period during the First World War, being used either at Herne Hill sorting sidings, as Victoria station pilot, or Stewarts Lane goods yard pilot, whilst 1602 had spent some time in its earliest career at Bricklayers Arms. Their most illustrious moments must in fact have been during the aforementioned war, when both were on His Majesty's Service, crossing the channel to France where they were used to shunt round the supply and ammunition depots at the port of Boulogne. When I became acquainted with them, they were almost entirely confined to shunting wagons from the "Green Yard" near the turntable to the coal elevator, and then being woken up every couple of hours to move a few more onto the elevator. In moments of extreme shortage, they did occasionally get upgraded to the Stewarts Lane goods yard pilot even at this date.

I never cleaned these two grimy souls but surprisingly I was once deputed to clean old 1302, when I had an odd hour still to complete my day's work.

Then come the large body of S.E.C.R. engines, the two largest numbers being the C 0-6-0 goods and the H class 0-4-4 tanks. Much has been written lauding the products of Drummond, Marsh, Urie and many other locomotive engineers of the former Southern companies but little in the way of tribute has been laid at the feet of Robert Surtees. Let me explain. The engines built between 1900 and 1914 were credited as the designs of H.S. Wainwright, the Locomotive Carriage and Wagon Superintendent of the S.E.C.R. His experience of locomotive design, however, was fairly limited and as a result the steam engines produced during Wainwright's term of office were actually designed in the main by Robert Surtees, the former Chief Draughtsman of the L.C.D.R, with artistic embellishments being left to Wainwright. As I was later to find, the engines produced were second to none and, as I was also later to find, much better than more celebrated engineer's products. As a personal opinion based on experience, the only engineer probably to equal or surpass him to that time was Adams of the L.S.W.R, so far as the Southern is concerned.

Several of the C class in particular had spent all their lives at Stewarts Lane. Then there were the express engines of the S.E.C.R, the E1 and D1 rebuilt 4-4-0s and a couple of E class (1514 and 1516) the latter the S.E.C.R. 'Royal' engine. Both spent most of the year dead in the depths of the shed, except during the height of summer, and looked very far from their former celebrated status. Then came six L Class 4-4-0s, of which I have mentioned 1764 as the first engine I cleaned.

There were also several S.E.C.R. N class moguls as well as the later Southern Railway produced variants of the same class, the most celebrated being the pioneer engine of the class, 1810, built in 1917. Concluding the S.E.C.R. engines were the R1 0-4-4 tanks, 1706 and 1710, that I mentioned in the first chapter.

The Southern Railway was represented by large numbers of the N15 class, better known as the King Arthurs and, in addition to N class moguls there were most of the U1 class numbered from 1899 – 1910. To complete the pre-war productions of the Southern Railway, there were three of the big W class 2-6-4 tank engines and a couple of the famous Schools or V class 4-4-0s.

The Bulleid products were, of course, the other fascinating exhibits and consisted of three of the powerful and pugnacious Q1 0-6-0 goods engines, and about a dozen of the light Pacifics of both the West Country and Battle of Britain classes. Although I admired the appearance and the reputed performance of these engines, they were in my first contact with them something of a pain in the neck – almost literally. Because they had no running plate to stand on to clean the boiler, a long high platform on wheels was provided, which with considerable difficulty could be trundled to the engine in order to reach the top length of the streamlined casing. The ladders which we used to clean the tops of tenders were not allowed, as the pressure could scratch the paintwork if leant against them. Cleaning the large flat areas of metal was a fairly tedious task as well, for the initial application of oil went to removing the dirt, and this was followed by going over the same area again to thoroughly polish it.

This just left the odd railway out as far as Stewarts Lane was concerned. The only examples of the former London Brighton & South Coast Railway stud shedded at Stewarts Lane were the E2 class shunting tanks, eight of them being there (2100 – 2107) the other two being at Dover. These then were the inhabitants, a total of about 120 engines.

I soon found that, although I knew them by class letters, many of the classes were identified by a generally accepted series of nick-names. For instance the L class were called "Germans" due to the fact that some of them had been built by the firm of Borsig of Berlin. The E1 and D1 classes were known as "Superheaters", as opposed to the unrebuilt saturated members of the classes. King Arthurs were simply known as "Arthurs" and the L1 class as "Glasshouses" due to their side windows (as a contrast to the windowless but otherwise similar L class).

The Maunsell U1 class were known as "U-boats"; I am not quite sure why, but have always fancied that perhaps it was because their chimneys looked very similar to the conning tower of one of those vessels, and fitted in nicely with the class letter. The L.B.S.C.R. C2x class were known as "Vulcans" because of their building company. The term "Spam Can", when I originally heard it, referred only to the Q1 class but it did later become loosely associated with the Bulleid Pacifics, though was not in general use as a term of identification. The S.E.C.R. R1 class were known as "Bobtails", which very adequately described the motion of them, particularly when running light engine, and a much later arrival at Stewarts Lane, the L.M.S. 2P 2-6-2 Ivatt tanks, were affectionately known as "Teddy Bears".

The shed itself consisted of the main shed, roads 1 to 16, which could take about six engines per road; then four outside roads, 17 to 20, commonly called the 'Sand-hole'; then the weigh house, with one engine usually standing outside its doors; 21 road, which led down to the side of Longhedge works; and 22 road, virtually detached from the shed, near the turntable, which held a couple of engines.

The main shed was very dark and ill-lit and even in daylight it took time for the eyes to get accustomed to the low level of light. To competently clean a black engine in a black shed was indeed bordering on the miraculous but somehow we managed to do so. I found interest in cleaning, taking some pride in the results and I think that, at the time, Southern engines were a fair bit cleaner than many of their contemporaries on other Regions. Yet as time passed, I began to feel some impatience that there appeared to be no move towards me getting onto the footplate. April gave way to May, still no sign, and then at last, some way through May, I was instructed to report for a few nights to the firelighters, prior to me getting footplate experience.

Engine cleaning is a fairly unenviable task but there are, or rather were, two jobs that I think were infinitely more unpleasant. The worst of all, I feel, was that of the boiler washer, whose job was to remove the plugs placed in various parts of the boilers anatomy, drain it and wash out the salts which had accumulated as a result of boiling so much water. A cold, wet, and thankless – but vital – task, but with what must rate as zero interest. Close behind that came the firelighters' job. At Stewarts Lane they were accommodated at the top end (i.e. furthest from the entrance) of 16 road. They had a couple of forms to sit upon and faced a furnace. Above the furnace was a opening placed above the end of 17 road, which usually had a wagon of sand standing under the hole. The furnace had a twofold purpose. Burning coals were taken from it to a 'dead' engine to light up the fire when necessary to do so. The firelighters also had the duty of shovelling sand from the wagon, onto decking above the furnace, and spreading it to dry. It was then fed into a hopper at the bottom of which was a small sliding door, from which firemen fed it into a bucket to replenish the sandboxes on the engines. There were two firelighters on duty and about once an hour they had to go round every engine in the shed which had a fire to keep the boilers filled, and put a few shovels of coal on the fires; this was in addition to their other duties which I previously described. The advantage of occasionally attaching a cleaner to one of them was that we thus got used to the rudiments of parts of the footplate equipment; learned the use of the water gauge and its drain cock to check water level and how to operate the injectors on all classes on engines etc. Also we discovered how difficult a seemingly easy task of getting coal onto the shovel, let alone successfully from the tender into the firebox, could be, much more difficult on a swaying footplate, I was later to find!

I could not recommend it as a lifetime's occupation, however. Most of the occupants of the post appeared to be ageing ex-firemen who had failed to get promotion to driver and had an understandably jaundiced view of life.

After my short stint with them, I was booked to go as third man on the footplate for six nights. I have no record of the date of my first trip but not unnaturally I remember it well, including the identity of the driver and engine, although I have unfortunately forgotten the name of the firemen who was so helpful and instructive, and is now probably a motorman on the Southern. The driver was Ernie Coles, a very likeable quiet man, who in later years in the top link I believe drove the first electrically-hauled 'Golden Arrow' with C class 1681.

On booking on duty I first had to learn the procedure to prepare an engine for service. Ten minutes were allowed for one to obtain from the display of duties the details of the days work. This printed list gave the following details: the class of engine, shed from which it originated, and timings and details of trains to be worked, as well as on some long duties, particularly shunting duties, times of reliefs of crews. The one detail particularly variable was, of course, the class of engine; most of the time the class designated was provided, but in times of shortage there could be some surprises. Note had to be taken also of any notices regarding speed restrictions or matters affecting working that had occurred at short notice. Then the engine number and its location had to be obtained from the running foreman and, having got this information, it was the firemans job to go to the stores at the rear of the shed. Here one got well and truly loaded, for one collected a firing shovel and coal hammer, a bucket, three headlamps and a handbrush, plus a variety of spanners. It was then a case of staggering to the engine and depositing these articles in their appropriate positions.

Having arrived on the footplate, there was a series of checks to be undertaken. First check the water level in the gauge glasses, next turn on the blower, open the firebox doors, go down on your knees and peer up inside the firebox to see that the fusible plugs were sound and not leaking any water. Then, providing there was sufficient boiler pressure, test that both injectors worked. Having progressed so far, there was now a sporting chance the engine was in fact fit for service; if something had been found wrong it meant another visit to the foreman to be directed to a replacement engine to which to lug the tools and start all over again. Then proceed to the front of the engine and check that the firebox door was securely closed. Having assured oneself of this it was back to the footplate and check that the three fire irons required were on the tender and safely secured.

Then began the heavy work. The fire was pushed over the box evenly and, with the bucket, one proceeded to a pile of shingle kept at the end of No.1 road and collected a few shovelfuls. Returning to the engine, these were spread evenly over the firebed, for at this stage the fire would be thin and the stones would come to rest on the bars and prevent clinker, when it formed, becoming a continuous mass over the bars, so improving air flow and hence steaming. To this day I can hear the crack of the stones as they heated and some of them split. Then came the task of making the fire up. How one made it up depended somewhat on the type of engine; with most narrow fireboxes it was built up to just under the firehole door and tapered to a fairly thin fire at the other end under the brick arch. On average it could mean shovelling in about a quarter of a ton of coal, although some shunting engines would require considerably less. I was to find out later, however, in the case of the Bulleid Pacifics, with their wide boxes, huge boulders of coal would be dropped in under the doors and about a ton of it could be used building on this foundation, making sure it was well up to firehole level, particularly round the back corners. Having depleted the tender of this amount, the next move was to go to the back of the coal area on the tender and shovel forward to the front until there was a mound of coal there. Then came a pause for breath while a search was made for headboards. On the Southern, unlike most other railways, due to the multiplicity of routes (particularly in the London area), engines carried white discs to indicate not what class of train they were, as on other railways, but what route they were working. As there were several hundred routes or combination of routes, the firemen had to carry a book which denoted these codes. Having acquired the correct number of headboards – and to do this sometimes required 'borrowing' from other engines in the shed – one had to be taken to the stores for the duty number, which took the form of paper numerals to be stuck onto the headboard. Returning to the engine, the last thing to do was to move to the water crane to fill the tender. There was little time to hang about to do all this in 45 minutes.

The duty I was to commence my footplate career with was the Chatham goods, from Herne Hill sorting sidings as far as St. Mary Cray. Here, at about 2 o'clock in the morning, we rendezvoused with a similar train on the up line which had come from Chatham, we exchanged footplates and, with another C class, worked back to London, whilst the Gillingham crew we had changed over with worked our former train down to Chatham.

As we moved off light engine from Stewarts Lane to run to Herne Hill sidings some three miles distant, the first thing that became apparent to me was the fact that I was going to have to acquire the railway equivalent of sea legs; as we sped on our way, I became aware of the sudden jerks in our motion as we passed over points or hit a rough rail joint, which in the first few unguarded moments threw me one way or the other. On arrival at the sidings, we backed onto our train of about thirty wagons of mixed freight. The guard had a quick word with the driver to let him know the number of wagons and to enter his name on the guard's journal. The railway is a traditional industry and at this point it gave me one illustration of this. Our guard was an old Brighton man, so instead of entering Stewarts Lane in his journal he wrote 'Battersea', the name of the long disappeared Brighton shed.

It was now my role to observe and keep out of the way. As we were hooked up to the train and waiting for a few minutes for the signal to clear, I installed myself on the fireman's seat, which was a wooden board fixed above the left-hand trailing driving wheel. The fireman opened the damper fully and turned on the blower just sufficiently to lift the smoke from blowing back from the doors into the cab. The safety valves started to lift as pressure reached 160 pounds, then the signal cleared, and we were off.

The start from the sidings and up to the middle of Penge Tunnel, over three miles distant, was all uphill, mostly on grades of 1 in 90 or 1 in 100 – heavy work for any locomotive, particularly starting from cold. The slowness of the start and the harshness of the exhaust was a complete contrast to our light running earlier. Now the fireman gave a quick pull through the fire with the pricker and turned the blower on harder, leaving it for about a minute to allow the contents of the firebox to heat up. Both the driver and fireman then worked as a team. As the fireman loaded the shovel and turned, the driver opened the firehole doors, and as the shovel was withdrawn so he shut them, for the suction of cold air through the doors was very noticeable, even where I was perched, and cutting it down to a minimum was essential. He fired four shovels towards the front. Immediately after starting, the safety valves had gone quiet and, about a minute passed through Herne Hill station, the noise on the footplate was terrific and sparks were now shooting heavenwards from the chimney. I expected the fire to be bright red but found it to have turned to a intense white, and very little detail inside the firebox could be made out due to the blinding brilliance of this light. The rhythm of the driver and fireman continued, with the driver also adjusting the cut-off and looking out for signals. At length we entered Penge Tunnel, some three-quarters of a mile long, and at last the fireman could relax a little as we gathered speed and the cut-off was brought back as we neared the summit. He put on the driver's side injector as we neared the top, for now the water was dropping rapidly down the glass, as the front of the engine started to dip downwards. We were gathering speed and, as the bark of the exhaust became muffled with the much lighter working, a rumble became apparent, echoed back to us by the tunnel walls; it was the sound of the wagon wheels as they gathered momentum. We burst into the open and the driver shut the regulator. Speed was about 30 m.p.h. and then came a snatch, as though a giant hand had hold of the train. This was the guard winding on his brake and we shot downwards towards Beckenham Junction. The extra injector was shut off now and gradually speed dropped as the gradient flattened out, the guard gradually easing his brake off. Just before the regulator was reopened, it was unusual to hear the clinking and clanking coming from the train behind as the wagons with their varying momentum ran into or away from each other; this is a sound you can only really appreciate if you are actually travelling on a loose-coupled train, as it can't be heard from the lineside. More heavy work of the same ensued, until at last we came to a halt in St. Mary Cray.

Shortly after, the up train arrived, and we changed over; then with the minimum of delay we were off again whence we had come, with another lot of hard work for the crew.

With dawn breaking we arrived back at Stewarts Lane, and then I learnt about the really unpleasant part of footplate work. Some railways employed firedroppers to do the work we were about to do, but the Southern policy was that engine crews should do everything pertaining to loco work, and I think this was right. Disposing an engine is a dirty job, but you do understand all as a result. The first thing as we ran toward the loco was to turn on a small cock on the footplate that ran a jet of water into the ashpan, to damp down the fine dust. On arrival the blower was turned on, and then round to the smokebox and open it. The Southern was behind all companies in labour-saving devices, I believe, no doubt due to the emphasis put onto electrification, and self-cleaning smokeboxes were completely unknown to us.

Smokebox ash is very fine, very black, heavy on a shovel but light when disturbed, so that it flies in all directions and is very hot. The smokebox has to be shovelled clean and, by the time the job is finished, quantities of ash can be down your neck and in your shoes. Following this task, the fire has to be cleaned or, if the engine is to be stopped for attention or boiler washing, thrown out. The latter task is the easier, for the fire can be allowed to burn down and it can be thrown out just before entering the shed road. Cleaning a fire is a much more exacting task. First the pricker has to be used to rake back the fire under the brick arch to expose the clinker in the far end of the fire box. This is then broken up and shovelled out, using the clinker shovel. The shovel is of iron and from six to eight feet long. With clinker 3 or 4 inches thick, removing it through the small aperture of the firehole and manoeuvering it round the cab takes some time to acquire the knack. On each successive entry of the shovel into the firebox, it gets hotter passing over the fire, so that a sponge cloth has to be used to protect the hands from heat. After the front of the fire has been dealt with, the fire is pushed forward and the back dealt with in a similar manner. On a hot day, it is a trying task. . . . Once done, the dampers are then opened and an ashpan rake obtained; you now go down into the pit, force the rake into the pan and pull out the ashes. It is another task where one can rarely win. If the ashes have not been sufficiently dampened, the resultant clouds of dust are in the eyes, ears and throat. On the other hand, if well watered, the contents run down the handle of the rake, covering the hands in a sticky wet mess. After this the tender is filled, coal taken from the elevator, the engine moved onto the turntable and turned for its next duty, then run into the shed. The remaining task is to refill the sandboxes from the sand hole, and then stagger to the stores with the tools. Having done this on my first trip, I realised the fireman's job had more to it than I suspected. For the rest of the week it was a repeat performance, except that for short periods I was given the task of attempting some firing on some of the easier stretches. The main problem I found was keeping my feet and getting the contents of the shovel into the place in the firebox they were intended to go. After the week was over, I returned to cleaning and awaited the next call. During the week I was summoned to the office where we booked on duty. A clerk then took me to a passageway outside the office where on the wall was a large printed notice giving all what would be now called the Health and Safety aspects of footplate work. I was solemnly enjoined to read them in his presence and, having done so, asked if I understood them. Having replied in the affirmative, I was told that I was now a passed cleaner, instructed to study the Rule Book with which I had been issued and told to return to work. I later found he had failed to tell me one thing which had some significance. As I was a passed cleaner and could be used as a firemen when required, it was part of my duty daily to look at the alterations list to see if I had been allocated to a job for the following day.

For the next week or so, my new-found status appeared to make little difference; I continued cleaning engines. Then one morning I came on duty as usual and was talking to my colleagues in the cleaners' lobby, when the door burst open and a driver peered through at us. "Someone here named Norman?" he enquired. I confessed that was my name. In none too polite terms he enquired where I had been and suggested it was time I was on the engine, as we were due off the shed in five minutes. In some confusion I followed him to a C class. Apparently I had been booked on the alteration sheet for this duty; when I had not turned up on the engine, he had done the unheard-of thing for a driver – he fetched the tools from the stores, having oiled up the engine. He made further enquiries and found I was a passed cleaner, and so came to look for me. I got on the engine, which I believe was 1583, I had no idea what the duty was or where we were going and, unusually, the engine was pointing engine foremost out of the shed. I enquired of the driver where were we bound. None too graciously he replied, "Empties to Maze Hill". Had he replied, "High street, China", I would have been just as wise, for I knew much of the Southern but knew not of Maze Hill. Before I could guess what next we were moving out of the shed; I just had time to splash some coal into the firebox and the next thing I knew we were buffering up to a train of ten empty coaches that had been hauled out by the Goods Yard pilot. To continue my confusion, we were going to work tender-first. We started away, heading up the severe gradient that led up the main line at Wandsworth Road, and on up to Clapham. Keeping my feet and firing engine first had been enough of a trial on the Chatham Goods, but running tender-first I managed several times to misjudge my swing and deposit much of the contents of the shovel onto the footplate. After Clapham pressure had dropped to 130 pounds but fortunately the regulator was shut there as we coasted down to Brixton, and then on towards Blackfriars. At the latter we ran round our train, recoupled and then away via London Bridge to Maze Hill. Eventually we arrived there, my frantic efforts managing to keep pressure just the right side of disaster, depositing our coaches in the siding. It was the first and last time I worked to Maze Hill in Greenwich, a most unusual working from Stewarts Lane. Thence we ran light engine back to the loco. From then on I kept my eye on the alteration sheet. . . .

CHAPTER THREE

The Herne Hill Link

A few days later my name appeared again and this time I was well prepared. It was a case of booking on at 9.30 on a Sunday night for 505 duty. The driver was Bill Miles, a rough and fairly fearsome individual at first sight, with little polish or finesse; later, when I had got to know him better, I found him to be an unpolished diamond.

We walked to Queenstown Road station pilot. This was an H class tank and, at this stage midway through 1948 (the date was 7th June), only six months after the railways had been Nationalised, most were still as the Southern Railway parted with them and the renumbering scheme had not yet been decided upon. The engine which was our charge for the night, however, had received a general repair since Nationalisation and, in consequence, in place of the usual SOUTHERN on the side tanks, was the inscription BRITISH RAILWAYS in full, but shaded in Southern Railway style. The number was s1184, the letter indicating, of course, that she was a Southern engine. For the first hour of shunting I watched the steam pressure gauge and the water gauge like a hawk, until at length I began to relax a little, Shunting makes only intermittent demands on the boiler and the frequent short pauses between shunts of vans or other light loads showed me that no great skill was required on a duty such as this. In fact I found that I had to concentrate more on other aspects of work. It was frequently necessary to tell the driver when the shunt signal my side was off, and learn that it was not a shunt signal but a 'dummy' to loco men. Of more variety was learning the shunter's handlamp signals. A white light swung towards and away from me indicated to pull away; waved across the shunter was to move towards him and, as the buffers neared to contact, he would hold the light steady, which was an indication to proceed very slowly and required a quick "steady" warning to the driver; red held steadily was, of course, Stop, which required a loud "Whoa!" to the driver. One signal I did not come across for some time puzzled me when I saw it – a red light raised and lowered several times; it turned out this was the signal to create vacuum or, in other words, release the brakes.

Another thing to assimilate was the geography of the station, Victoria being, of course, one of the biggest in the country and, in reality, then (as to some extent even now) it was two stations combined. Platforms 1 to 8 were the Eastern Section of the old South Eastern & Chatham, and from 9 to 19 were the Central Section, the old London Brighton & South Coast portion. We had relieved the pilot on the Central side, and the shunter here was responsible for the shunting of his section, as well as the signalling being the responsibility of the Central side signal box. There was also an Eastern side shunter and signal box.

We were busy throughout the night, for there was much shunting of vans for the early morning newspaper trains, for parcels traffic, and gruesomely enough for the small hours – a traffic which has gradually departed from the railways – one funeral van (containing one corpse, male, on this occasion I was reliably informed, returning from the Continent to I have forgotten where). After we had completed our shunting for the time being on the Central, we started work on the Eastern side.

We were very busy, for on a Sunday night only one Pilot was provided as against two on all other nights. We got about a 40 minute break, which gave us a chance to have something to eat and replenish the engine, as well as taking water. At last, just after four in the morning, our work complete at Victoria, we ran home light to Stewarts Lane. I had to dispose of the engine and so home in the dawning light to bed. I felt I had achieved something and was very much happier than after my Maze Hill experience.

From that date, from time to time I was booked for firing duties but in the main they were shed duties only, preparing and disposing engines, backbreaking work and not too interesting. There were also a couple more Victoria pilot jobs plus a shunting turn in the goods yard at Battersea Park. The latter was an interesting place, because it was adjacent to the former L.B.S.C.R. locomotive shed, which had closed with the electrification of the Brighton Line. The roundhouses were (and are) in existence, being at that time used for parking Southern road vehicles. The goods yard was extensive, one side being to the south of the Brighton line and the other being sandwiched between the line and the River Thames. Most of the traffic was inter-Regional traffic from the London Midland and return traffic back to them, with the Southern trains working in the main to Norwood Junction, Three Bridges and a few other Central section locations. At this time, I had not kept a log of engines and dates that I had worked on them but I remember this particular day well, for the driver I worked with was a real gentleman of the old school – neat and clean as a whistle, and very mild of manner. His name was Beauchamp, and he was soon going to retire. We had many pauses from shunting whilst trains came in and out of the yard, and it was fascinating to hear him talk. He was an old Brighton man and had actually in his youth fired Gladstones but, although he had an affection for the Brighton, he did not think the good old days were all that good. He related how, when he was a cleaner, they had to make the engines really shine, being responsible entirely for certain engines. He told me of an occasion when one of his mates had been fired on the spot, when having reported to the foreman cleaner that he had completed cleaning an engine, the foreman inspected it, rubbed his hand *underneath* the tender, and found some spots of dirt.

Earlier I described the locomotives at Stewarts Lane, but now I was getting to know the personality of the depot, which in its way was as varied as the individual engines. All personalities are different, of course, but due to the history of the railway, this was expressed by the attitudes of the men concerned. Most of the drivers had been employed by the pre-Grouping companies in their younger days and most, of course, were ex-South Eastern & Chatham men but when the L.B.S.C.R. depot had closed at Battersea, only half a mile away, nearly all had been transferred to the Lane. They formed a sizable minority. The S.E.C.R. men saw them initially as interlopers and the resultant lack of welcome made the Brighton men feel out of place and on the defensive, particularly as few of their engines came with them. In the course of time, these attitudes softened but to some extent they still remained and jokes with barbed edges sometimes surfaced.

The Chatham men considered the Brighton a pretentious and autocratic system; in turn the Brighton men tended to look down with a superior disdain on the Johnny-come-lately Chatham. My own conclusions eventually were that the Chatham was a more humane concern than the Brighton and, although there is much to be said for tradition, the Brighton suffered by having a bit too much of it.

In September the summer timetable came to an end and this signalled a reduction in work of considerable proportions on the passenger side, with many locomotives being put into store at all depots for the winter. It also, at the same time, brought a new roster with it. In such a roster most men moved down a bit but it also gave an adustment to some who were waiting to get a rostered position. I was surprised and delighted to note on a preliminary display of the roster that I was being rostered as a Fireman in No. 13 link from 11th October.

I found on enquiry that No. 13 was known as the Herne Hill link, as it was principally engaged in manning the shunting engines at Herne Hill Sorting sidings, about three miles away. In addition, however, there were a number of other local duties, as well as some main line engine preparation and disposal duties. These also involved taking locos to Victoria, or bringing them back from that station.

Five o'clock on the morning of 11th October saw me booking on for 67 duty, and I met Harry Ward. Harry was my first rostered driver, a tall, thick-set man in his late 50s, with a surprisingly low, melodious voice. He had originally hailed from Kent and in his early firing days had worked on the S.E.C.R. steam railcars on the Elham Valley line. He was a slow, easy-going character, who I understood had some kind of unspecified medical complaint which debarred him from anything more ambitious than shunting and light engine duties. Tragically, some years later he was to die in the cab of an electric train in which he was travelling home, in a collision near Barnes; he was, I understand, burnt to death.

The duty on which we were engaged for the week certainly was by no stretch of the imagination strenuous. After preparing our C class, we trundled round the loco picking up odd vans, one of which might be the sponge-cloth van for Ashford. The sponge-cloths were issued to enginemen for two purposes, there being a rough one, which was intended for a variety of tasks, for instance holding hot fire irons, cleaning engine windows, wiping drops of oil after lubricating parts of the engine etc. The other one was a fine one, which was for wiping the hands and face, usually used at the termination of a duty. The laundry for these was at Ashford, and a van was allocated to each shed to convey them. The sand-hole wagon was another picked up now and again, and wagons were also collected from Longhedge works. The biggest collection, however, was a large number of empty coal wagons from the 'Green Yard' which had been emptied by the coal hopper the day before. Having collected these together, we then hauled them out of the loco, past Stewarts Lane signal box, and back into the goods yard, where we picked up the builders' merchants, coalmerchants', and any other wagons, and then moved the whole cavalcade (without a brake van; very novel in those days) off to Battersea Yard, the guard riding with us on the footplate. Here we shunted our trains, sorted out the return load, and then took on about an hours ordinary shunting, acting as the relief for the yard pilot – they took the hour for a meal break, and for servicing the engine.

At about 11 o'clock we pulled our return load back to Stewarts Lane, disposed of the engine (not a very great task in view of the very small mileage covered) and went home – hardly a turn to set the world on fire. On this first day I came across an old friend, however, No. 1681, which you may remember was my C of the first footplate trip.

It would perhaps be tedious to state the number of every engine on every day that I worked on but just to give an idea of the sort of variation, the engines for the rest of the week were; 1714, 1681, 1683, 1576, and 31582. The renumbering scheme had now been started but, as will be seen, only one engine had been renumbered that I worked on during that week. I had decided from the outset of getting a rostered position that I would keep a record daily of my work, with details of the driver, engine, duty, and anything of note that occurred. The observant may also notice this means working six days a week. In 1948 the guaranteed working week, Monday to Saturday, was 44 hours, which meant that there was only one rest day every two weeks. Sundays were not part of the guaranteed working week, that is to say the company did not have to employ on the Sunday unless they wished but roughly every other Sunday everyone was rostered to work, so that in practise we worked a six-day week.

The C class goods engines, as well as being competent, moderately powered freight engines on the road, were useful to shunt with, as this type of duty showed. The South Eastern engines were all equipped with a short double-handled regulator, which was excellent to use on the road for grasping with both hands to open the main port when maximum power was required very quickly, and was also very easy to use (because of its light nature) when shunting. The masterpiece for shunting work, however, was the Stirling steam reversing gear inherited from the S.E.R. It had two hand levers to operate it. The first one was either pushed forward or moved back, and the second moved from the horizontal to the vertical. This second lever, when moved to the vertical position, allowed steam to enter a piston mounted alongside the engine boiler, and push the valve gear in either the fore or reverse direction, dependent in which direction the first lever had been placed. The travel of the gear stopped immediately the second lever was put back to the horizontal position. The gear was then held in position by a second hydraulic cylinder mounted under the steam cylinder. The action of this reverser was very quick, and took a little knack in getting use to. It, was, in fact, so fast that any small delay in closing the steam valve could take the engine from forward to reverse gear with the regulator open – not a practice to be encouraged! It took about a maximum of two seconds to go from full forward to full reverse gear. This was therefore a very much quicker and less exhausting exercise that using a lever or wheel type of reverser. The same type of reverser in modified form was introduced by Bulleid on the Q class and on all his subsequent designs. The only disadvantage the C class had for shunting work was the brakes. They had the vacuum brake, which was no match for the sharp application and quick release of the straight air brake fitted to the Brighton engines, and as later fitted to the diesel shunters.

So ended my first rostered week, a very easy week's work. If it had been a case of early rising, then the following week was even earlier, for on the Monday morning it was a question of booking on at 3.10 a.m. I don't know who thought of the excruciating times we had to book on, but I am convinced of two things; the first is that in many cases they could have been better arranged, and the second, the instigators of such times did not have to work them! We walked the half mile to Battersea Yard and relieved on the pilot, shunting until 6 o'clock, and then running home light to depot and disposing the engine.

This was my introduction to the E2 class of shunting tanks, and the engine we had on this turn was the pioneer one of the class, 2100 – the first engine to be built for the L.B.S.C.R. by L.B.Billinton, emerging new from Brighton works in 1913. They were very different in footplate layout when compared to the S.E.C.R. engines I had up to now worked. The first difference was that the positions on the footplate were altered, the fireman's position being on the right-hand side, which was also generally the case on most of the engines built by the Southern Railway and its other constituent companies (the S.E.C.R. being the odd man out in this in that the fireman's position was on the left-hand side). At least we became adept at firing from either position! The Brighton also went in for two other arrangements foreign to the S.E.C.R. Many of its engines were fitted with water condensing apparatus, which took some of the exhaust steam after it had passed through the cylinders and returned it to the side tanks. As the level of water fell in the tanks, this could cause the temperature of the water to rise quite considerably and it was sometimes quite unpleasant opening the tank lids when water was taken, as clouds of quite hot steam would gush out and the lid handle got quite hot. The normal type of injector cannot use heater water but just will not function, so that a special type of hot water injector was installed on the fireman's side. This pump gave a slow and very definite 'clonk' every time it pushed water into the boiler. When I started working on the class, only 2100 and 2101 were equipped in this manner, the other members having had two S.E.C.R. type injectors fitted with the condensing apparatus removed at the same time.

The Weir pumps in fact worked very well – which was just as well, for the hot water injectors could never be got to work. The first three engines of the class were fitted with lever type reversers, which were well balanced, and I supposed had been so designed due to the extensive shunting duties the class had been built for; with the right hand it was easy to lift the catch and throw the lever forward or pull it back. The later engines, however, were fitted with a screw reverse, which had an air cylinder to reverse it. To operarate this power reverse, a small cock situated by the screw was turned. It was wise to stand clear of the flailing arms of the reverser when this was operated, for they were turned several rotations per second and, as it was located at about hip height, getting in its way could cause contact with a very sensitive part of the anatomy which left one doubled up for some time. Most footplatemen only made the mistake once. This disadvantage apart, it provided a very quick and easy reversing mechanism. The firedoors again were completely different from the Chatham style. The S.E.C.R. had sensible doors which slid to and fro by pulling the lever attached to them, and had a small flap at the top to control the small smount of air it is sometimes necessary to allow to enter the firebox to aid combustion. The Brighton firedoor was an oval one with a catch which had to be lifted, acting like a catch to a gate; it could then be swung open. The middle of the door could also be opened separately, as a solid oval plate which could engage on a ratchet. The theory was that firing could be done through this smaller hole, but in practice, because of the small number of engines we had with this type, we always opened the door.

The firebox was quite a deep one and could be well filled and left to look after itself for long periods, leaving the fireman to concentrate on maintaining water level as well as looking out for shunters' signals. With the door to the cab closed, a spring-loaded wood seat was swung down from the bunker and, so seated, one could watch the world go by. The regulator was a long one with arms both sides of the centre screw. When it was closed, on the driver's side the arm, about three feet long, had the end at about shoulder height, whilst on the fireman's side it was a couple of feet from the floor.The intention of the design was no doubt good, in that standing looking out from the footplate, the regulator could be grasped from either side, without losing sight of the shunter. One thing I fear had been overlooked. Most of the time the driver had control of the regulator, and with heavy shunting it could be in the fully open position and then smartly closed. On the fireman's side the arm would come down from the high to low position very quickly, and, as I found by personal experience, if the fireman was bending down shovelling coal to the fire, his rear end was in exactly the right position to receive an unexpected (though perhaps not always undeserved) whack of chastisement.

The brake was a straight air brake, which gave a very powerful application, and was almost ideal for shunting. I say almost, for it was so strong that if too heavy an application was made shunting a heavy load, it could cause a wagon coupling to break like a twig. A small application had to be made until the couplings tightened;then a full application could be made. The pump for the air was mounted on the front of the tank on the fireman's side and he also had to control the steam supply to operate it.

My first couple of hours at Battersea yard gave me a chance then to get used to this class, which over the next six months in particular I was to work on, for they were usually the ones which were used as the Herne Hill pilots. In fact 2100, as well as being my introductin to the E2 class, turned out in the fullness of time to be the engine on which I logged the highest number of individual day's work on a single locomotive, a total of 26 days in all; this was eventually closely followed by a C class, No. 1575, with two days less.

After we had stowed 2100 in the shed, we disposed a visiting W class tank engine,31925 of Hither Green, and prepared an Arthur, 776 *Sir Galagars* for service, and then staggered wearily home.

The line from Holborn Viaduct in the City of London joins the main line from Victoria at Herne Hill, a distance of 4½ miles from the City terminus. Half a mile to the north of Herne Hill station was situated Herne Hill Sorting sidings, covering a total area of 14 acres, and bisected by the Holborn line. They were called the sorting sidings, for goods trains from Eastern Region hauled by J52 or N1 tank engines of the former G.N.R. brought transfer goods to Herne Hill, as did the original Midland Region.

Here the pilots sorted them to their various Southern destinations. The foreign engines arrived on the down side of the yard, then ran clear of the train; next, the Southern pilot was attached and pulled the train up, the brake van was detached and was then taken by the visiting engine to the side sidings, where it attached the van to a returning train, and so away. In the meantime, the down side pilot would have shunted the train into various roads being made up for different parts of the Eastern Section. The trains from the other Regions arrived at all hours of the days, except that all goods movements on the suburban areas on the Southern were absolutely prohibited between 7 and 9.30 in the morning, and 4 and 6.30 in the afternoon, due to the intensive electric service. The busiest time was between midnight and six in the morning, the quietest from late afternoon.

On the up side, trains arrived from many different parts of the Region and were then formed up for mostly the other two Regions, but there was a certain amount of reforming of Southern traffic as well. The up side pilot was a good deal less arduous than the down side. There were two pilots in use, for much of the day. The down and up pilots left Stewarts Lane loco coupled together at 9.30 each night, except Sundays, and ran bunker-first, light engine to Herne Hill sorting sidings. Both remained working there until 2.45 pm the following day, when the down side pilot worked a short trip goods to Clapham, and then on to Stewarts Lane, and so back to the loco, arriving there at 4.21 pm. This left the up side pilot to work both sides as required until 9.30, when it was despatched a mile up the Holborn Line, to Camberwell, to couple onto the brake van of a Southern train from Hither Green and haul it back to Herne Hill. It then worked a train of empty wagons to Blackfriars, ran round them and worked them to Walworth Sidings, where they were left to be filled the next day with the refuse from the householders of Camberwell, Walworth and other nearby places; we had the honour of working these loaded wagons of well-perfumed garbage back to Herne Hill and, having left them in the welcoming arms of the shunters, the engine ran light to the loco.

This meant that the down side pilot was away for about 19 hours from the loco, whilst the up side was away for 27½ hours, returning to the loco at about one in the morning. This long stint consumed a lot of coal and oil, so that it was essential the bunkers were well stacked when leaving the loco. There had to be a couple of firecleaning periods during the day to remove the worst of the clinker as well.

Prior to the E2s at Herne Hill, the shunting had been undertaken by the T class. Their bunkers were only half the capacity of the E2s, carrying a total of a ton and a quarter, which would have allowed an average consumption of less than a hundredweight an hour, and it was the custom before leaving Stewarts Lane to fill the firebox to capacity and have hardly any standing room on the footplate in order to have enough fuel.

On the following day, therefore, I was introduced to the Herne Hill scene by working on the down side pilot (74 duty). This required us to book on at 4 a.m. and travel passenger on an empty stock working to Holborn, then by electric to Loughborough Junction station (which was in fact nearer to the sidings than Herne Hill) and relieve the night crew at about 4.45. On this first day, the engine was 2103, and as the week progressed I became familiar with the type of working and the arrangements that I have described. The old adage that cleanliness is next to godliness was a maxim held to be very true on the footplate. It might be thought that, as the job was a dirty one, care was not taken in keeping things clean but this was very far from the truth. It was the fireman's task after firing to use the handbrush and sweep the footboards clean. The cab windows had to be cleaned, while the boiler water gauge glasses and their armoured glass protector, provided to prevent flying glass fragments should the gauge burst, had to be cleaned when the engine was prepared and also before getting relieved. On this duty we got relieved at about 11.15 a.m. and about fifteen minutes earlier it was the custom to stop shunting. First the general cleaning and tidying up the place, then a thin film of oil was poured over the top of the boiler front. Due to the heat, this rapidly ran down, giving a thin coat over most of the surface. The coal watering pipe was next turned on, taking hot water from the boiler and, while standing away from the footplate one thoroughly sprayed the front. The resultant mixture of hot oil and water took any residual dust away and it dried in a few minutes, leaving only any brass or brass fittings to be polished to a shine. Then the tool bucket was filled with warm water from the injector overflow pipe and both driver and fireman, with the additional help of soap, removed any dirt from themselves.

Woe betide any crew that got relieved on a dirty engine; however rough the trip, they would have a long time to live it down.

So the week went by with different engines of the same class being used on the remaining days. The week following was one of nights, again on the up side pilot. This was the turn we ran light engine from the loco coupled to the other engine. I had not bargained for our speed between Brixton and Herne Hill, having been used to about 10 m.p.h. maximum whilst shunting; this time we must have touched all of about 50. With 4′6″ driving wheels, this was going some and the resultant lurching and swaying had me hanging on to the cab side somewhat grimly.

Goods shunting was a lot different to the sedate performance I had experienced in moving fitted stock about at Victoria station; fly shunting, that is loose shunting of goods wagons, is vastly different. As for as possible once shunting of wagons to various roads has started, the skill lies in knocking the wagons off and stopping short of the points that next have to be changed by the shunter; this saves the shunter considerable time and work, for he does not have to give additional hand signals to move the wagons back, as well as saving reversing the engine. It is not always possible, but if the driver does not succeed most of the time inevitably he is made aware of the fact by a few well-chosen words from the shunter. I found I had to learn a modified command, for as well as forward and back, when we had to fly shunt, the shunter either gave an exaggerated swing of his arm in daylight, or at night the same emphatic swing of his signal lamp. The command to the driver was then, "Hit em up!" and he responded by giving full regulator, bashing full tilt into the wagons. Then on my "Whoa!" he snapped the regulator shut and applied the brake. The drag of the load on the engine was quite violent and it took a little time to get ones shunting legs, to prevent bruises.

On our first night we had 2101, a unique engine so far as Stewarts Lane and the Southern Region was concerned, for she was still bedecked in the old Maunsell type of livery, with the squashed SOUTHERN painted along the top of the side tanks and the huge two foot high number on the tanks. She was the only remaining engine at the loco not to have the smaller shaded Bulleid-style numbering and the last tank on the region to retain the old Maunsell style at the time she was eventually repainted in 1951. It had lasted well, for she had the old style applied in October 1939.

Later in the week, however, there was another surprise. Without warning I did my first bit of driving. It was completely unexpected, unauthorised, and nearly ended in disaster. Harry had just left the engine, having been told we would not be moving for another five minutes, and he had gone to the shunters' cabin some distance away. Hardly had he gone, than an engine entered the sidings, having crossed from the down side. It was unable to back onto its train as our own engine was standing foul of the points over which it had to pass.

Immediately to the rear of our engine was a 20-ton brake van. The shunter came up to me. "Move back a bit to let him onto his train", he said. I was about to say that I couldn't drive, when I felt the devil sidle up to me. I'd seen it done scores of times now; there really wasn't anything to it. "Right-o, mate!" I replied calmly, my heart pounding away. I moved the brake handle to the release position and heard the sigh of air as the brakes came off. In true style I opened the first port of the regulator and we hurtled backwards. The couple of feet between the engine's buffers and those of the brake van were covered rather more rapidly than I had anticipated. I groped for the brake handle but before I got hold of it the buffers contacted with an almighty crash. Fortunately the brake van kept on the rails but hurtled back into the darkness. Meantime I found the brake handle. As I did so, however – consternation! The brake van had hardly started on its precipitous way before there was another loud crash! It had contacted a line of empty wagons a few yards further on. Now I gritted my teeth as it bounced off them and rebounded back towards me. The engine was now stationary but again the buffers clanged and the engine shuddered as the brake van made contact. After a couple more softer return cannonades, everything came to a stop. I sat down in a cold sweat, realising there was more to driving than I imagined. The shunter fortunately had gone back to the other engine, so that my virtuoso performance had been heard but fortunately not seen.

The next night, instead of the usual E2, we had something completely different. The loco had run a bit short of shunting engines and borrowed one from Hither Green. I could hardly believe my luck, for we had none at Stewarts Lane. There she stood, her outside-frame tender displaying springs above the running board, an 01 class goods 0-6-0, No.1430. She had been built to James Stirlings designs for the S.E.R. in 1897 and rebuilt with a domed boiler in 1913. They looked, so far as the engine was concerned, like a small version of the C class, although the footplate was noticeably narrower and the vacuum brake was of an older pattern, being a Dreadnought. The tender looked really ancient with its outside springs and handrail, being also much lower pitched than a C class. It was possible to look right over the top when running tender first, instead of round the sides. In motion there was a noticeable difference, for the exhaust was a very throaty sound compared with the sharp bark of the C. We found 1430 to be reasonably good for shunting, the only real disadvantage being the lower brake power. It was also decidedly cooler than the cab of the tanks, not such a good thing at night. We had her again on the following night before she was once more returned to the fold at Hither Green.

The several weeks that followed were in the main spent on the Herne Hill pilots and included the down side night turn, when we spent the whole time just keeping pace with the incoming tide of trains hauled by G.N.R. or Midland tanks. Most of the traffic was coal, with a sprinkling of bricks or general goods traffic.

During the day there were a couple of times when we ventured out from the sidings to Camberwell signal box, which lay about a mile to the south. Here we hooked up to the brake van of a train which had either come from Hither Green or was the returning Crystal Palace (High Level) goods. When the shunt signal cleared, we gave a crow whistle, which in turn was answered by the train engine at the other end, and then both engines opened regulators in unison to begin the haul up the stiff gradient towards Herne Hill sidings. It was on this short run that the limitations of the E2's boiler became evident, for by the time we reached Loughborough Junction station some three-quarters of a mile after starting, steam would have dropped from the maximum of 170 to about 130, and here the injector would be put on, causing the pressure to plummet further, saved only by the fact that almost immediately the regulator would be shut as we approached the sidings. The boiler was based on that provided for the L2 4–4–2 passenger tank engines which came out in 1908, and lasted only little over twenty years, due largely to the total inadaquacy of the boilers. Certainly this was borne out by our limited experience of them on the road. It was an adequate shunting engine boiler, but nothing more; my sympathies went out to the old firemen who worked the L2s.

Christmas Day dawned and, as it did, we ran light engine home from Victoria to Stewarts Lane at 6 a.m. on 2101. Then, running railways was a 365 days-a-year job and, although there was a reduction of service on Christmas Day, trains ran to all parts and we had plenty of shunting of vans and coaching stock through the night. The following week, the last of the year, found me having come full circle in the roster of 13 link, for I was back on 67 duty again. This time it was with another 01 visitor from Hither Green, No.1381, which we had all the week and added variety to the usual E2s with the occasional helpings of C or H class engines.

In looking back over the old year, I felt that, after the uncertain start at Stratford, I had become established in a job that interested me and at last was getting the hang of it. I looked forward to what the New Year might bring.

CHAPTER FOUR

The Norwood Goods

A new roster started on 9th January and I eagerly scanned it to see if I had moved up to another link. Disappointment – I was still in 13 link, with Harry Ward, and so we started on another three month stint. Throughout this period it was much the same thing as before but a couple of interesting variations on the theme occurred. Towards the end of January I worked the down side pilot turn which in the afternoon saw us working the Clapham Goods and for all of that week I had charge of a third man, whom I had to show the ropes. His name was Victor Steele. It might be thought gratifying to have someone to do your work but, in fact, showing how to do a job, if properly done, can usually be harder than doing it oneself and three on a footplate is a little crowded, particularly on a tank engine. I remember Vic Steele was fairly happy with most of the job but did blink a bit when the 'donkey' – that is, the Westinghouse brake pump – stopped working and I had to restart it. It had the stubborn habit at times of running short of lubricant and sticking, so failing to maintain the necessary reserve of air for the brake. This was not always noticed until pressure had dropped to a very low level and it became a matter of some urgency to restart it, in order to be able to stop!

On the Clapham Goods we ran from Herne Hill to Clapham on the up main line, for a distance of about two miles. On arrival at Clapham, we propelled back across the down main, into a shunting neck, and then down into the small goods yard. The load was at most about six wagons, all coal except for an odd one for a builders' merchant. On this particular day, as Harry applied the brake to come to a stand on the main, it only gave a soft application and we were glad of the additional assistance of the guard's brake. Looking at the air pressure gauge, pressure stood at about 30 pounds per square inch instead of the normal 90 and a stolid silence issued forth from the pump which sat ahead of the side tank on the fireman's side. I ushered Vic Steele aside and swung myself out, working along the inch width of running board that led to the front. It was not thought to be a good idea to hold up the main line, so as I worked my way with a large spanner in hand along my precarious foothold, Harry released the brake and gently opened the first port of the regulator, pushing the train back gently toward the shunting neck.

On arrival at the pump, I gave it two or three hefty blows on the cylinder head and it came to life, clonking merrily away, causing air pressure to mount in time for our application in the neck. Nowadays I suppose we would be retrained from such a practice by the Health and Safety act, but in the rashness of youth, and its strength, we dismissed the possibility of falling to the ground, or – worse – to an electric conductor rail!

By the beginning of February, another loco shortage was upon us; 2102 and 2104 had been dispatched to works for overhaul and, as a result, a C class (1578) was provided as a substitute; during the month I fired it ten out of twelve consecutive turns on the Herne Hill pilots, a somewhat draughty time of year for such capers.

I suppose one of the attractions of loco work is that the routine is often broken by the unexpected. Early in March, we had a spare turn. This is when the roster merely books a time of attendance and, if either the driver or firemen are required for a duty, they can be booked into any turn two hours either side of that time. If no duty has to be covered, then it is a case of booking on at the time and being available to cover the duty of a man failing to report, or being used to prepare and dispose engines. On this day, Harry had been booked to cover another driver's turn and I had been left spare, having been teamed up to carry out preparation and disposal duties with a driver named Harris.

It had been a busy duty, for I had prepared 34084 of the Battle of Britain class, to work 'The Golden Arrow', then disposed two ex-S.E.C.R. engines, N class 31812 and E1 1506. I was just recovering my breath when the running foreman came into the lobby yet again and I gave an inward groan as he made for my driver once more.

"Dispose that one on the coal road, and then you're finished," he said, fumbling in his pocket to find its number. "35017",he announced. All thought of tiredness vanished. A Merchant Navy, all of which were shedded on the Western Section. *Belgian Marine* had been one of the Pacifics used in the Exchange Trials of 1948. It was most unusual for one to visit our Section, let alone our shed. We found that she was still attached to the black eight-wheel tender that had been fitted to the engine from a W.D. 2-8-0 to give greater water capacity during the trials. Disposal in fact took little effort, as she had obviously worked only a short distance, lodging at the shed for a time prior

The E2 class tanks were the mainstay of the Herne Hill pilots. These two views are of 32102 and 32103 awaiting return to us at Stewarts Lane shed after overhaul at Eastleigh works, August 1952.

No. 1371, an 01 class goods engine, complete with old outside-framed S.E.R. tender, photographed in 1948. **Below:** *0-6-0T No. 756* **A.S. Harris** *awaiting breaking-up after finishing her days at Stewarts Lane.*

to going on to works. Just prior to this I had been officially notified that I was appointed a fireman. The only practical use of such notification was that I would no longer have the prospect of being returned to engine cleaning, which was a relief, for as a full-time occupation it had little attraction.

So another three months went by in the Herne Hill link, with work concentrated on the E2s. Now and again, Harry would entrust me with a little driving and I got the knack of applying the Westinghouse brake without breaking too many couplings. The air brake was, in fact, so powerful that, when fly shunting a heavy train of coal, if the brake was fully and continuously applied, the strain in the loose link couplings could be such that the heavy snatch could part a weak link.

During this period there were no engines of particular note that I worked on, except for a couple of days when an 01, No.1380 of 1893 vintage was loaned to us. At the end of March, another roster list appeared. This time I had been promoted and jumped two links up into No.10 link, the Norwood Goods. On my last week in the Herne Hill link there were a couple of interesting visitors in transit to the shed. The oldest was a Stroudley D1, No.2299, which had not seen active service for years. Adorned in the old mid-thirties style with her number in big numerals on the side tanks, she was in a very woebegone state, her smoke box had rusted through to a hole on the left-hand side, through which the blast pipe could be glimpsed. Officially she had been withdrawn from service over twelve months previously, and she was dumped at Stewarts Lane for a few days before being towed to works to be broken up – a very different sight from that day in 1876 when she emerged spick and span from Brighton Works as No. 36 *New Cross*. The other engine was also another formerly named engine of the Brighton, which during the late war had the unique distinction of bringing down a German fighter. This was D3 0-4-4T 32365, previously named *Victoria,* which was visiting Longhedge works for some minor attention. In November 1942 this engine was attacked by a German fighter near Romney Marsh. The plane flew so low that a wing tip touched either the dome or cab roof and, as a result, crashed in a field. The engine had extensive boiler damage due to cannon shells and machine gun bullets but the crew escaped, in that respect being luckier than the German pilot.

On 2nd April 1949, Harry Ward and I were on duty for the last time, working on a somewhat larger engine than we usually did, 34074, a Battle of Britain class. We ran the Pacific back from Victoria off a boat train working and disposed her.

Getting up at 1.30 in the morning to go to work can be said to be a little trying and a number of duties at Stewarts Lane required early rising. Such was the case on 4th April 1949, when I worked the Mottingham milk turn with Ernie Coles and C class 31716. This duty booked on at 2.50 a.m. and consisted of working light engine to Clapham Junction, then the morning milk train to Mottingham, about a mile east of Hither Green. After this, it was light engine to Ewer Street, a small depot used to service locomotives situated between the fruit market and the Metal Box factory between London

Bridge and Waterloo stations.

We only used it to reverse round the curve and onto the bridge over the Thames at Cannon Street. There were two lines on the west side of the bridge used to hold locomotives waiting for incoming trains, and it was possible to look down on the river below and watch the then busy river traffic, mostly tugs towing a string of barges. We had the benefit of about an hour's stand, which gave me time to make the tea in the signal box, a long low building at the north end of the bridge, with two signalman working like beavers at that time of the morning.

After this break we headed a train of empty stock to Stewarts Lane sidings, reversing on the way at Ludgate Hill, which had been closed as a passenger station for many years. Before the electrification of the Kent Coast lines, there were many of these empty stock workings to either Rotherhithe Road (R.Road for short), Grove Park, Blackheath, and Stewarts Lane to berth the commuter trains from the Kent coast, with return workings in the afternoon.

The following morning I slept blissfully on, despite the alarm clock, and awoke at about eight o'clock. I should have worked my first Norwood Goods link duty with my new mate Bill Godwin;instead I presented myself at about 10 o'clock to the Shedmaster to express my apologies and to obtain permission to resume duty the next day. The privilege of booking on at 2.30 a.m. was taken seriously in those days, for if an interview was not obtained by midday, in one's own time, permission would not be granted to work the next day.

I looked forward to working the Norwood Link, as it consisted of working goods trains from Battersea Yard to Norwood Junction, as well as other Central section work, and to date I had not worked over this part of the line. Indeed, I had not worked any heavy goods trains of the type that were commonly worked to Norwood, which could load to 40 or 50 wagons. To work these trains, Stewarts Lane was provided with three of the W class 2-6-4Ts, numbered at that time 1912, 1914, and 1915. The road too was a challenge. It was steeply graded throughout and had a number of junctions which had to be worked through as quickly as possible to avoid delays to the surburban electric service. Starting from Battersea Yard, there was a slight down grade for about a quarter of a mile, followed by the curving up-gradient below the well-known façade of Hamptons depository, climbing above and alongside Stewarts Lane loco to Longhedge Junction. Here there was a slight fall, then a short sharp climb up to Pouparts Junction, and so on to the Brighton main line. Passing through Clapham Junction the real collar work began, with a long hard haul up to Balham, where the main line was left, and then up another steepening grade past Streatham Hill electric depot to the junctions before West Norwood. This last part of the trip had to be taken gently on the curving down grade to prevent snatching of the couplings, which might easily cause a breakaway. In sight of West Norwood platform, with the couplings taut, full regulator would be the order of the day and the 2-6-4T would roar through the station up the long grade to Gypsy Hill, the severest climb on the journey. Just past Gypsy Hill station is the tunnel, in which the summit of the climb is reached. The tunnel opens out at Crystal Palace Low Level station, where yet another junction takes the right-hand curve to Norwood Junction, the left being for Lower Sydenham. Because of this junction, under the home signal approaching Gypsy Hill was a distant signal, which when "On" indicated that the junction at the other end of the tunnel was "blocked" and that therefore the Gypsy Hill starting signal would be cleared, which allowed steam to be kept on, for stopping here even in dry weather could mean a battle to get away again. Once Crystal Palace had been passed, the line dropped sharply for a mile and a half, which required holding the train back all the way down, ready to stop if need be at the home signal for the goods yard.

The return journey from Norwood Junction was always via Selhurst and, apart from the climb from the yard to Selhurst station, which was about a quarter of a mile, was down hill, along the Brighton main line all the way in contrast to the down trip. The up run, unlike the down, was – as far as the fireman was concerned – a matter of watching the scenery of South London pass by. This then was the new route, with a new driver, and a new (to me) class of engine.

Booking on at 2.30, the duty entailed preparing the 2-6-4T for service (for which an hour was allowed) and on the morning of 6th April I arrived in good time, the Running Foreman telling me that the engine for the turn was 1912. I made my way to it and started work; meanwhile my new mate Bill Godwin arrived. He was a craggy, stocky individual of dark compexion, in his early fifties, and an old Brighton man. Over the next few months I got to know Bill well; he was a good competent engineman, a staunch defender of the Brighton.

The Stewarts Lane W class engines were of the original batch built at Eastleigh and differed in several respects from the later Ashford-built examples. Unlike them, they were right-hand drive and had gravity sanding operated by a large lever on the fireman's side, which he had to pull to and fro frequently when required. They were also of some historic interest in that they were fitted with the original tanks and bogie wheels from the ill-fated River class. These looked like the W class in many ways and had been rebuilt as the U class 2-6-0s, following the bad derailment due to unsteady running at Sevenoaks in 1927.

A little before our booked time, we started away from Battersea yard. I was a little apprehensive as to my ability to maintain a sufficient head of steam to Norwood with such a heavy load and such a large engine. Soon after we had started, however, I realised what a remarkable engine the W class were. They were never much in the public eye due to their almost exclusive use on goods workings, but as we started away, the firm even torque of the three cylinders made itself felt, as the engine quietly but firmly got hold of the train. Seemingly with little effort and no fuss, we were on our way. The even, persistent draught, six beats every revolution of the wheels, quickly drew on the fire without pulling it from the bed, and soon the red turned to white hot. I watched the pressure gauge like a hawk, and found it rising to near the 200 pounds maximum. Putting on the injector made little difference, the pressure held, and water consumption was not excessive. Little and often was the firing maxim, keeping a thin fire at the front and well up under the doors. When we hit the top of the gradient at Gypsy Hill, pressure under quite a pounding dropped to 170, the lowest on the journey, with water well up the glass. After this came the braking down to Norwood Junction. This too was impressive. We had no tender brakes to assist of course but, as well as brakes being fitted to the coupled wheels, this was one of the few classes in the country that was fitted with brakes on the bogie wheels, a powerful graduated steam brake, which was master of the train. I never looked back on the W class from then on; in all I did 44 days work on them, without a single rough trip, a record that cannot be claimed for many classes.

Although the Schools class was considered to be Maunsell's most oustanding engine, I think that the success of his basic N class formula has not been fully recognised except perhaps by those who have worked on them.The N class boiler was a very free steaming one and was used on a variety of classes as well as the N, namely on the N1, U, U1 and W. The front ends of all these classes were well designed and gave a definite punch of power that transmitted a surge of purpose through the engine and right through to the man with his hand on the regulator. The W class, as I have intimated, were tailor-made to work heavy, tightly timed goods trains, whilst the N class were two-cylinder engines, having the same driving wheel size as the Ws, and were at their best on heavy goods trains, although in the summer they were pressed into passenger service. They had no trouble in coping with up to ten coaches, but this was definitely not the ideal job from the engineman's point of view. On one occasion I worked 1810, the original engine of 1917, on such a train. We went down Sole Street bank at about 70 m.p.h. and the rattling of the cab against the side sheets of the boiler was deafening. It had to be heard to be believed; and one simply had to hang onto the seat, as the bucking of the footplate decreed it was the last place for that part of the anatomy. On the other hand, the U class with 6′ wheels were very steady riders, even in excess of such a speed and were the ideal passenger engine of the type; in my experience they were the best steaming of all the classes. The U1 class, however, were a different kettle. They, like the U class, had 6′ wheels but in addition had three cylinders. This made them powerful, but the greater demand on the boiler and the tendency when worked hard to tear the fire caused steaming to be less reliable, and water consumption to be noticeably higher. On the flat and up hill they were considerably faster than the N class (though not as fast as the U) and they were not the smoothest riding engines. In the main they were used on passenger trains from Stewarts Lane, although a certain amount of goods work was undertaken. In 1949 Nos. 1890, and 1900 – 1910 were at Stewarts Lane. The only class that I cannot claim to have had extensive experience of was the N1 class. There were only six of these, a three-cylinder version of the N class. I only fired one, 31878, a Hither Green engine. It steamed badly, had excessive water consumption, and was a thoroughly bad lot as far as I was concerned, although this may have been due to its run-down condition, also my inexperience of the class.

The week following my first run to Norwood, I was rostered for a turn which involved working parts of two duties, which gave a contrast of working on an express engine of bygone days and a modern express engine. The first part (783 duty) was on a Brighton Atlantic; the second (427 duty) a Bulleid Pacific. Quite a contrast, but they had one similarity; both had wide fireboxes mounted over the trailing carrying wheels.

783 duty booked on at 2.00 p.m. preparing the Atlantic for service, then at 3.00 p.m. working light engine to Eardley sidings, via Clapham Junction. Empty stock was then worked from there to Victoria tender-first, which formed the 4.50 departure for Tunbridge Wells West. Then the engine was worked to the Central side loco sidings at Victoria, where the fire was built up and the coal shovelled forward on the tender, to back down onto the infamous 6.10 p.m. to Uckfield. We did not work the train, however, as we were then relieved in the platform, and then took over an up Ramsgate train, which arrived at 7.07. After the empty coaches had departed, we worked light engine back to Stewarts Lane, disposed and then prepared the engine, finally working it back to Victoria in time to be relieved just before its departure at 9.35 p.m. to Ramsgate.

On the first day the Atlantic was 2426 *St. Albans Head*, still in Southern Railway malachite green, and shining to perfection, the work of the Newhaven staff – her home shed. The neatness of this design was remarkable, an improvement on the original design that hailed from Doncaster. The visual layout was very satisfactory and care had been taken to give a well laid out and comfortable footplate. The ugly parts of locomotive equipment were not allowed to mar the outline of the finished product for, like all Brighton engines she was Westinghouse brake fitted, but the unsightly pump was concealed beneath a trap door in front of the smokebox, behind the buffer beam. Making up the fire was alike for both old and new. A big fire was made up at the back of the box, and especially round the back corners, with very little in the front. The significant difference was in volume, about half a ton in the case of the Atlantic, and over twice as much in the case of the Pacific.

The Pacific on the first day was 34089 *602 Squadron*. This meant shovelling about a quarter of a ton of ash, clinker, smokebox ash and a couple of tons of coal (a ton or more in the box, plus a ton from the back to the front of the tender to ensure adequate supplies on the run).

The following day, an even more gratifying sight awaited. The Atlantic this time was one of the first Brighton series, 2038, an H1 class, in the only post-war repaint of the class in Southern green. *Portland Bill* to my mind was an even finer looking engine than her larger sisters.

The Atlantic firedoors were the typical oval ones of the Brighton (and even of the G.N.R.), with a blackout door which could be placed in front of them, provided during the war and retained on them thereafter. As we pulled into Victoria with the 4.50 empties, Bill asked me with obvious pride, "Well, what do you think of her?" In reply I didn't enthuse but merely said I thought she was not bad – in fact, I had found she was very free steaming and running and had the edge over her younger sisters. As for looks, I can hardly believe even in L.B.S.C.R. days she can have looked any better than in her present condition. The following day it was 2038 again and then the turn reverted to 2426.

A few weeks later, I worked on another famous Brighton class, this time an I3 tank engine Nos.2025. Again, it was only a round-the-houses turn. They were a much bigger engine than the Atlantic tank wheel arrangement suggested and the spacious cab was a revelation; it was possible to stand practically upright on the big end of the inside cylinder motion when at bottom centre without touching the boiler with the head, and this made it a very easy engine to oil up for the driver.

To this date, then, I had worked on engines of two of the major pre-Grouping companies of the Southern, but not on an engine of the largest company, the former London & South Western Railway. Unknown to me and unexpectedly, however, that was soon to change.

On 30th May we booked on at 4.50 p.m. for a fairly mundane shift, but somewhere someone had blundered, and we were in for a far from mundane and a somewhat extended shift. The duty as rostered required us to work the Victoria station pilot from 5.50 until 10.06 p.m. On this day it was H class 1261 and, after being relieved, we were rostered to take over from the crew of an up Tunbridge Wells train, working the engine back to the shed, disposing it and then booking off duty at 12.50 a.m.

When the train ran in it was, unusually, hauled by a D1 (No.31745) instead of the normal U1 Mogul. On arriving back at Stewarts Lane, however, we were met by the running foreman who told us that we should have been booked on later for the duty and then have relieved on special Duty A at Clapham Junction (Western Section). He asked us if, under the circumstances, we would leave the D1 for someone else to dispose and go to Clapham Junction to relieve on the special. We decided to do so, the special being a train from Eastleigh to Selhurst electric depot routed from Clapham Junction via Herne Hill, Tulse Hill and Streatham Common. We made our way to Clapham Junction and waited in the shunters' lobby for the arrival of our special. We were told it was running late but at length we heard the slow unmistakable exhaust of a London & South Western engine.

Stepping out, we saw the train consisted of T9 class 30281, from Eastleigh shed, followed by eight brand new, green electric coaches, formed by two 4-car SUB units (which were being built in large numbers at Eastleigh to replace the old pre-grouping stock that had to continue in service through the war years). At the rear was a goods brake, for no power brake was available on the stock. A more incongruous introduction to the famous "Greyhounds" could hardly be imagined. We slowly chuffed off from Clapham Junction with our unbraked load and, as we ran down the gradient towards Longhedge Junction, I took a look, as far as was possible in the dark, at the unfamiliar footplate. The L.S.W.R. type firedoor akin to that fitted to the King Arthurs was no stranger; the pressure and vacuum gauges were also standard. We passed Longhedge Junction, over the top of the shed on the elevated line that took us to Factory Junction. Bill closed the regulator as we came round the curve, looking for the home signal to see if we were signalled onto the main line from Victoria. I decided to put on the injector at this point but looked round for the water feed control in vain. It was not situated on the tender as on South Eastern engines, or under the fireman's seat, as on most Southern engines. Having drawn a blank, I asked Bill where the water feed control handle was and was thunderstruck to be told that I was standing on it! The handle was placed just about where the fireman stood when firing, to be kicked open with the foot. I had always understood that Drummond was a foremost engineer but this gave me cause for doubt, for could there be a more idiotic place to put the water feed, where the fireman was likely to either kick it or trip over it when firing. Certainly a number of times during this trip I caught my foot on it, inadvertently knocking the injector feed off and having to restart it.

In addition to this hazard, instead of the doors which closed off the gap between the engine and tender, there was only a chain, of fairly thin gauge, which could be attached to a hook on the tender and, as it was at my waist height, I could visualise myself tipping base over apex across this chain and out onto the permanent way. There also appeared to me to be the hazard of losing one's footing when firing and not having the solid doors for support, for on occasion this could happen.

The home was off, so the regulator was opened and we started to climb the grade past Wandsworth Road. With this heavy load, progress was both slow and noisy. Eventually we breasted the top of the gradient at Clapham and lumbered on at a slightly faster rate towards Brixton, but again this soon settled back to a snail's pace as we climbed towards Herne Hill. Beyond there the line ascends for over a mile up an elongated S with a ruling gradient of 1 in 60, flattening out in Tulse Hill station platform. Many times a day empty stock from Victoria to Eardley sidings tackled this gradient and, even with much more powerful six-coupled engines, sometimes slipped to a standstill on the climb. They were usually rescued by bringing up the next electric passenger train and, with the engine pulling and the electric pushing, eventually got to the top. There was certainly no hope, therefore, of a four-coupled engine at so slow a pace getting to the top unaided and we chuffed our steady way into Herne Hill station to grind to a halt at the starting signal. While Bill went off to telephone for assistance, I scrambled over the coal and looked down into the stygian depths of the water tank. We had none too much. Probably water had last been taken some hours before at Basingstoke so, whilst opportunity presented itself, I lifted the bag of the nearby water crane into the water hole and turned the crane on. In pitch black or dimly lit places, we were provided with a primitive but effective means with which to pierce the darkness. This was the flare lamp – a small, round metal pot about the size of a mug, with a handle and a spout. Cotton waste was fed down the spout, leaving a couple of inches protruding. The pot was then filled with paraffin, making a bright and easily portable lamp.

Bill returned with the news that one of the sorting sidings pilots was going to bank us up the hill. I had hardly turned off the water and put the tank lid back on before the E2 came onto the back, billowing smoke and with the safety valves hissing. The direct loaded valves on our own engine were now going full blast and we were ready to go. A crow on the whistle, and an answering crow from the banker just to complete the cacophony, and we were off. The wheels on our own engine ground hard against the rails, the feeling that becomes a familiar indication that adhesion is at its maximum just before a slip. So the regulator was shut but, with the considerable amount of steam in the steam chests and superheater, it was too late to stop the slip and, sure enough, the driving wheels spun and the coupling rods rattled until the power had been expended; then the regulator was reopened again. The engine was worked heavily but gradually speed increased with the able work being done by the tank at the rear, and soon sparks were shooting skywards at both the back and front of the train. Even so, the top of the bank saw us down to about ten miles per hour, for here was the worst part, as the bank turned right up to the station at Tulse Hill, and we had a number of half slips until we gained the flat ground in the station. Here the banker shut off steam and drifted away from us to return down the hill. We now got a mild run on but could not go too fast, for stopping the weight behind us would take a considerable distance should we sight adverse signals. I kept firing little and often through the unfamiliar doors way down at floor level, compared with the higher sighted boxes I was used to, giving a curse now and again as I tripped over the water control handle. I peered anxiously at the steam and water gauge at frequent intervals, for the type of working we were engaged on took plenty of both. At last we passed through the spur at Streatham and down onto the Brighton main line. Here it was again heavy working as we made the continuous climb on the down line to Selhurst – three miles of collar work.

The sky was lightening as we passed the Selhurst starter and dropped down to the left of the main into the electric depot. We unhooked and dropped down to the outlet signal to return tender-first on the main line via Clapham Junction and back to the shed via Balham. Relieved of our load and with quite a big fire, the safety valves hummed away non-stop, for little steam was now needed as we ran down off the North Downs towards home. In complete contrast to our pedestrian progress, we were now hurtling along at 60 or 70 m.p.h. with the regulator shut, tender-first. No more work, so I sat down for a quarter of an hour until we stopped at the shunt signal to run back into the shed as dawn was breaking. Twelve hours of unusual work and so home wearily to bed.

There were no more great surprises that week, a U1 was on the Tunbridge train for the rest of the week, except for the last day when 30534, a Q class 0-6-0, appeared. They were used on these trains from time to time, the class being Maunsell's swan song, actually making their appearance after he had retired. I had a few turns on them but never got to like them; the steaming was none too brilliant and when steam was shut off the tender would bounce to and from the engine, giving a most uncomfortable ride.

June 1949 was a quiet month, with no surprises, and most of it was spent back on the Norwood trail with the W tanks. Towards the end of the month we had a week of working to Kensington with H class tanks to pick up J.Lyons cake vans and milk tank trains; half the week we had 31554 and the other half 31177. On the Monday a new roster had been published, which showed that the following week I was to be promoted up one link to No.9 link.

In celebration of this event, Bill let me drive one trip a day back from Kensington, which was very enjoyable, for he was not a driver who let his mates have much access to the regulator. And so, on the 25th of the month after stabling 31177 in the shed, he and I said goodbye. Some years later, however, Bill was destined to be the last driver I worked with on the Eastern section.

CHAPTER FIVE

Round the houses – and down the main

My new driver was none other than Fred (Dobso) Smith. Smith of course is the commonest English name and at Stewarts Lane we had been blessed with three gentlemen bearing this name. I was destined to have two of them as my regular mates, the aforesaid Dobso and, at a much later date (Two Gun) Fred Smith. I never discovered why my new mate was commonly known as Dobso and I'm afraid it must now forever remain a mystery.

I do know how Two Gun Smith came by his nickname. Apparently in his youth, when a fireman, he had an addiction for guns and was wont on the footplate to wear two air pistols. This eventually had tragic consequences, for the tale goes that at sometime, when he had been relieved at the end of his duty, the fireman that took over from him was examining one of the pistols and looking down the barrel when he inadvertantly pressed the trigger. This resulted in the loss of an eye. Needless to say, from then on the guns were discarded forever, but the nickname stuck.

In fact it was not strictly correct to say that my new mate was Dobso Smith, for indeed I was seldom to work with him, as the new link I was in was a 'Spare' link, which had usually only a booking-on time without any rostered duties.

This particular link was apparently intended to cover the lower links, which was in the main "round-the-houses" duties moving empty coaching stock, and local goods as well as shunting duties, for a much more exalted link was No.2 link, the main line spare link. I was therefore resigned to working a variety of none too spectacular duties, still, the advantage was that there would indeed be considerable variety. The disadvantage was that on some days there would be no running turns to cover and I would be confined to the dirty disposal and preparation jobs, or there would be the occasional day when there was little to do but sit in the lobby waiting for something to turn up, enlivened only by chat of present or bygone days, or a game of cards.

In fact it did turn out to be something like this but I was to find that some turns a bit higher up the links were covered from time to time and I had failed to take into account the effect of the summer service, which put an almost intolerable strain on the resources of both men and machines at the shed, particularly at weekends.

The first three weeks were certainly "round-the-houses" turns, as well as working engines to and from Victoria; this involved working on 13 H class; 4 U1 class; 2 C class; 2 D1 class; 2N15 class; and one example each of the E1, Battle of Britain, Q, 13, L and N classes – a grand total of 29 engines in 18 days (three days being Rest days or Sundays). This was with a total of six different drivers, none of whom was my rostered mate.

On 18th July, I was covering the job of a fireman, who was sick, on a quite mundane job, Battersea Yard pilot, on unusual hours, a turn starting at ten in the morning. It was quite a pleasant shift for, although there was a fair bit of shunting to do, there were now and again pauses of ten minutes or so, whilst we waited for trains to leave the yard, and as the yard was situated between the South Eastern and Brighton main lines, the passing trains could be viewed, as well as the procession of empty stock and light engine workings passing between Stewarts Lane and Victoria. My driver was Jimmy Nunn, a grand character who suffered with a bad chest, not an ideal affliction for a footplate man who liked smoking. At about five in the afternoon we worked the engine, E2 tank 2104, light back to the loco, and disposed of her. Before going home we made our way to the office to see the alterations clerk and find what turn we would be booked for on the following day, Jimmy also being spare on the morrow. The clerk told Jimmy that he had booked him for the Ferry vans from Battersea Yard to Dover Marine but had not as yet been able to book a fireman for the job. With that, Jimmy asked about booking me. And so I was booked up for my first main line trip. The sun was shining all the brighter as I made my way home!

After the war, with the restoration of passenger services in full to the seaside resorts, plus a considerable increase in Continental traffic, including B.A.O.R. leave trains, as well as a reasonable amount of freight traffic, the demand for locomotives at Stewarts Lane during the summer timetable was very considerable, and any extra calls were hard to meet. The Continental ferry van traffic ran as and when required, and was not run daily. The traffic consisted of French S.N.C.F. and Italian F.S. fruit vans which were run onto the specially equipped Southern Railway boats enabling the Continental stock to run right through. Despite the vans being empty, the train was in fact a heavy one, for the unloaded vans were allowed to accumulate until a full train length was ready to return. The duty was No.429 and was booked for a

King Arthur departing from Battersea Yard at 10 a.m.

I arrived at the shed a good thirty minutes early the following day, going first to the running foreman to enquire the identity and location of the engine. Expecting to hear him quote a familiar number, probably an N15, I was astonished to be told "77355". Making my way to the road beyond the coal hoist, I beheld a class of engine I had not seen at Stewarts Lane before, a War Department 2-8-0, a rare beast indeed on the Southern. It was an unusual sight in its peeling army livery with the B.A.O.R. shield between the letters WD on the tender and a liberal coating of rust and grime. All the motion and coupling rods were encased in filthy grease. I very soon found that it was as mechanically sound as it looked. I had hardly mounted the footplate when a crew came to the L class which was standing behind my engine. The driver came up and asked me to move the 2-8-0 forward to release his engine. I wound the reverser forward, heaved open the long regulator, and we made a shuddering forward movement. I had cleared the points and the engine behind followed. When signalled by the fireman of the engine, who was standing at the points, that I had gone far enough, I found that there was no need to apply the brakes, for the friction in the boxes was such that we came to a stand without any artificial aids! At least the clanking from the motion had also stopped.

I then trundled back to whence we had come and set about preparing the engine. The Southern Railway had been loaned a total of 42 of these big 2–8–0s at the end of hostilities to ease the shortage, but by this time most of them had gone into store, at far-flung places throughout the Region, and were awaiting works; they were all shortly afterwards transferred to other B.R.Regions. On the Southern they were known officially as the AY class. Not only were engines at this time in short supply however, for so was coal. The contents of the capacious tender of 77355 consisted entirely of briquettes, coal dust compressed into brick-like slabs, in which was etched the name of the manufacturer. Surprisingly, although not up to the standards of best Nottinghamshire coal with which Stewarts Lane was supplied, it was not a bad fuel as I was to find on this and on some subsequent trips. Whilst making up the fire I was joined by Jimmy Nunn, who was also not greatly enchanted with our mount. Eventually we trundled off light to Battersea Yard and it was noticeable that as soon as the regulator was shut, speed rapidly fell off. We backed onto the vans, about 40 in number (being empty they counted as 30 loaded). Promptly we started away towards Dover. It was obvious from the outset that we were going to have a rough ride; everything clanked, creaked or groaned – and we were booked non-stop at an average speed of 35 m.p.h. for the 76-odd miles to our destination, this with driving wheels of 4′8½″. . . . Other things beside the riding were to give us some surprises. The first of these was shortly after starting; as we climbed up past Factory Junction I had just put on the injector, when Jimmy asked me to look out for the advance starter at Wandsworth Road, as we had late clearance of the home signal. So I peered out of the side window and was hit in the face by a fine stream of water. On recovering from the surprise, I saw that it was shooting from the base of the screw mounted on top of the injector clack box, which was sited on top of the boiler to the rear of the chimney, just nicely catching the slipstream to spray the area outside the window. At first this was an annoyance but it was a fine hot summer's day and, as the journey progressed and I got hotter, I found that it became a cooling facility that I availed myself of from time to time. However, the streaky effect of water, sweat and coal dust on my visage has to be imagined to be fully appreciated. I found the fire box quite long and a real swing of the shovel for the front end corners was needed. After a bit I had misjudged some of the throws and was building up a fire to a hill just under the brick arch but use of the pricker levelled the mountain, pushing it to the front. I learnt that these locos liked a thick fire at the back of the box but the front had to be fairly well supplied, to prevent cold air being pulled up to the tubeplate. Steaming, in fact, was not at all bad and I managed to keep pressure from dropping below 190 against the maximum of 225. At Herne Hill we joined the route that I had previously passed over as third man on the Chatham Goods, and so on through Penge Tunnel, Bromley South and up to Bickley Junction. The lines from London Bridge and Victoria converge there and the gradient thereafter drops down towards St Mary Cray. We passed through the station with the distant 'on' and approached the junction home signal. Jimmy had shut off steam and, as we drew nearer, he gave a small application of the vacuum brake. No response. A heavier application resulted in a slight tug from the train. Jimmy gave maximum application and hastily moved the engine steam brake handle to the fully on position as the signal loomed nearer. After a series of disconcerting jerks from the train we at length came to a stop, with the signal alongside the cab still at danger. Examination of the train provided us with the answer to this alarming episode. Most of the vans were in fact fitted for operation with Westinghouse brake and, although a through vacuum pipe was fitted, only a handful of vehicles were fitted with the brake. It was fortunate that we had discovered this before the descent of Sole Street bank some 15 miles ahead. At length the signal cleared and we were off again. I had heard of the terrors of Sole Street but, of course, that was in the up direction; since we were going downhill to the valley of the Medway I expected no surprises – but I got them. I was actually glad to see Sole Street station, for my arms and my back were starting to tell me what main line work was all about. Shortly beyond the station the regulator was shut and I sat down thankfully to enjoy the descent to Rochester. We gathered speed to about 40 m.p.h. before the fun began. As the big ends went forward the engine tended to run away from the tender; as they came back the tender caught us up, the result being an almighty resounding bang every time it did so, which was of course every revolution, or three hundred and fifty six bangs to the mile in our case, for over five miles. In turn the coal was tumbled forward in the tender by this action and, as it filled the hole I had excavated by my exertions, it started to overflow and cascade onto the footplate. Eventually the floor was covered; the flow continued and started to fall under the cab doors and away onto the permanent way. By the time we crossed the Medway we had a full boiler, full head of steam and footplate full of coal. For several of the succeeding miles I did my firing from the floor and not the tender!

On we went through Chatham and up the climb to Gillingham, then through the undulating Kent countryside, until at last we sighted Faversham. Here we took the right hand fork of the junction to Canterbury and Dover. I now ached in every limb and at last I felt my strength ebbing. In desperation I noted that steam pressure was down to 160 pounds and water half way down the glass. Sensing this, Jimmy Nunn told me not to worry as soon he would be shutting off to run down to Dover. Thankfully I sat down and we started to coast down the grade towards the port. By the time we clanked through the tunnels of Dover Priory and then into Dover Marine station, everything was back to normal; I was certainly glad to have arrived. We left the 2-8-0 in Dover shed and, in fact, I never saw her again. Later she was renumbered 90254 and went, I believe, to Eastern Region. Surely a more untypical introduction to the South Eastern main line could not be imagined. This was the first and last time I ever fired a WD or, for that matter, an eight-coupled tender engine. We had a novel return as well, for the next train back to London was the Golden Arrow. Of course, two coal-begrimed footplatemen could not expect to travel back in the passenger comfort of this renowned train, but Jimmy knew the guard, so we travelled back in the guard's van. This was the only time I ever travelled in such style; it was fascinating looking back through the full length glass observation panels at the receding track and instructive to see lines of dumped WD 2-8-0s in various sidings awaiting works!

A little later in the year I was booked to work my first passenger train. I certainly experienced a thrill of pride when the regulator was opened on U1 31890, as we worked this train away from Victoria (Central) on a ten-coach special for Lingfield races. The route for Lingfield was all uphill to East Croydon, where there was a short break in the climb, and then the ascent began again as soon as the station was passed. The Brighton main line was left at South Croydon, and the gradient up the North Downs began. It culminated with the entrance into Oxted Tunnel, after which came a breathtaking dash down through Oxted to the foot of the Downs on the south side and so to Lingfield some nine miles further on. I found 31890 steamed well and ran fast, though riding fairly roughly over points and bad patches of permanent way. I had not been beyond Selhurst before on the Central section, the furthest point in working the Norwood Goods, and the Oxted line was a delightfully rural and scenic route to work over. We ran down into Lingfield with the smell of hot oil from the front end, always noticeable to me on the 'U-boats' after working hard. Here we watched our load of hopeful punters disembark. I always found considerable satisfaction in observing passengers leaving a train I had worked at a terminus, it gave a feeling of achievement; this was the first time I had done so. Afterwards we took water and then shunted the train into sidings, for later the train was to work on to Brighton, as there were no turning facilities at Lingfield. We in turn changed over to an up special from Brighton which was worked by a crew from that shed; they had a U class, brand-new out of the works following a general overhaul. She looked a treat shining black in her repaint. 31890 was, in fact, an interesting and unique engine of the class, for she had originally been built by the Southern Railway in 1925 as the sole example of the three-cylinder K1 class 2-6-4 tank and was then named *River Frome.* Following the derailment at Sevenoaks in 1927, *River Frome* ran special tests both on the L.N.E.R. and on the Western Section of the Southern Railway under the control of Sir Nigel Gresley, where it was found to roll so violently that the Southern Railway board decided to rebuild them all into 2-6-0 tender engines. There is no doubt that the side tanks were the cause of the trouble for, although the U1s could be lively, they were not dangerous in the rebuilt state and the U class were rock steady. There was one detail in which 31890 varied from her sister. The running plate rose over the cylinders instead of being in a straight line; in addition there was a cover over both the outside eccentric links to protect them as they protruded through the frame.

Our new charge on the up side which we now manned was 31613. This was the first U class that I had fired, for they were strangers to Stewarts Lane, most of the class being concentrated on the coastal sheds of the Central Section or on the Western Section at this time. They were thus a rarity for us. What a treat an engine newly out of works was – an engine and a half to what they were after a few months in service! I found that I had only one problem working back – trying to keep the pressure down to stop the safety valves blowing off all the time. She ran like a deer and I am sure if fired with newspapers she would still have steamed like a good'un. Arriving back in Victoria, I had had a novel and happy day's work; I almost thought I should have paid the company for the enjoyment.

Now and again, Dobso and I found we were actually working the same turn. He was a most likeable man, slight of build and stature, with a witty, happy disposition. I was sorry that we got so little opportunity to work together.

Many weeks of shunting and local goods followed, then towards the end of the summer timetable I was booked late turn on a Sunday to work three lots of empty stock trains to Eardley sidings. The difference about this turn was it was booked to use a light Pacific, which had previously worked up from the Kent coast. Up to now I had only worked any of the large express engines to and from Victoria to Stewarts Lane, mostly light engine or now and again hauling empty stock. As the distance was just over a mile, however, this could hardly be called firing experience. I was at last going to get some real experience of them. The engine when it ran in was 34077 *603 Squadron* of the Battle of Britain class. My mate was Two-Gun Smith on this occasion and, after the train had been taken off us we ran light to the Eastern side carriage siding in order to go on the turntable there, so that we should be running engine first on the empties out of Victoria.

Eardley sidings were extensive, being used to store some daily stock workings for the Central Section but in the main they held coaches for excursions and specials. They were situated about half a mile from Streatham station and could be conveniently reached from the Central section, from a steeply-graded flyover, which leaves the Brighton main line just south of Streatham Common station or from the Eastern Section by mounting the steep grade from Herne Hill to Tulse Hill, as previously described in our adventure with T9 No.30281. This latter route was very difficult, for usually the engines used were Moguls and, even with these powerful engines, a twelve coach train in slippery conditions could result in them stalling and requiring assistance. King Arthurs were not permitted, due to the sharp curve at the top of the gradient in Tulse Hill station, which was a bit too much for their wheel base. Light Pacifics were allowed, however, but were rarely rostered for such humble workings.

I built a big fire up on 34077 and sweltered in the hot evening air. It was my first chance to savour some hours on one of Bulleid's footplates. Shutting the Ajax firedoors completely hid the fire; it was as though it had completely vanished. The firedoors I personally think were one of Bulleid's happier notions. They minimised the amount of cold air admitted into the firebox, always being structured to completely close once the manual was released and also they ensured that heated secondary air entered the firebox to aid combustion. They were also fitted with a small steam cylinder, which was operated by a treadle. By touching this with his right foot on turning, the fireman could cause the doors to open as he swung the shovel round to deliver its contents into the firebox. Immediately this was done, as he moved back, a slight lift of the foot caused the doors to close. It took a little practice to perfect the technique and once I regularly fired the class, I invariably used it. In the main however, most fireman did not trouble to use it, instead opening and closing the doors using the manual handle; thus a useful facility was largely wasted. The other much appreciated innovation was the provision of electric lighting. A Stone steam generator was mounted under the footplate on the fireman's side, turned on by means of a steam cock controlled by a large handle on the same side of the footplate. All the steam pressure and brake gauges were illuminated, as was the reverser gauge, water gauges and, under the footplate, the injector overflow pipes. Compared with the sole light given by the paraffin water gauge lamp on other engines it was paradise. In addition, the headlamps were electrically lit, as were those also provided on the back of the tender for tender-first working. After dark therefore it was the custom to light only one of the paraffin headlamps, so that it was handy for use as a red tail light for light engine running and also available as a danger hand signal should the need arise. Comfortable tip-up seats were provided, plus adequate cupboard space for tools, reefer jacket or overcoats. The tender back completely shut off the coal space from the footplate, except that a large oblong trap door was provided which could be opened when the engine was being prepared, and large lumps of coal could be helped through the door onto the footplate in order to make up the huge fire it was customary to carry on these engines. A water sprinkler was also available on the tender front; this was operated by a cock on the fireman's side – useful in keeping the dust down.

A Hither Green-based example of the magnificent W class 2-6-4 tanks, No. 31921. **Below:** *QI class No. 33036 on the 9.50 a.m. Victoria-Eardley Sidings empty stock train passing Balham. The author is just visible in the cab; 6 June 1949.* *[Photo: K.G. Carr]*

No. 35026 on 21 Road at Stewarts Lane with superheater elements being renewed. The far bridge is the connecting line between Longhedge and Factory Junctions, the nearer one being the South London line which passed over part of the roof of the shed.

13 class 4-4-2T No. s2025 at Oxted, as fired by the author. [Photo: K.G. Carr]

The driver's job in oiling was also simplified. Outside the engine he had only to oil the outside big ends, coupling rods and crosshead, a matter of eight points; all the rest was accomplished by filling large trays on the firebox front which delivered oil by connecting pipes to the various locations. The cylinder lubrication was by means of mechanical lubricators mounted under a trap door in front of the smokebox but the responsibility for filling those lay with the shed staff, as did the topping-up of the oil bath for the motion. This was quite a considerable task, so that they were not the shed staff's favourite babies, particularly when much of the equipment they had to get at was concealed by the airsmooth casing.

We backed onto the first empty train of the evening, which was routed via Tulse Hill. With a full 280 pounds on the clock and the safety valves roaring, we started away. One of the well-known drawbacks of the Bulleid Pacifics was their propensity for slipping. They were certainly fairly light on their feet but, by and large, the fault lay with lax driving methods, as I later had the opportunity of finding out. The driver was provided with a steam chest pressure gauge; on opening the regulator, the pressure would mount from zero and continue to climb as long as he left the regulator open, until it was within 5 or 10 pounds of boiler pressure. To do so when starting off was very ill advised, for pressure could go up to about 270 pounds per square inch and, if slipping then started, even if the regulator was shut, there was a vast quantity of steam that had got past the regulator valve and would continue to slip the wheels until exhausted. The correct way to start was to open the regulator, whilst carefully watching the gauge. Once it had got over the hundred mark or so, shut it; at the same time one felt through the handle how the wheels were responding. Also one could listen to the exhaust, for the start of the wheels beginning to lose adhesion could be felt and heard. Slipping could certainly be avoided; the only time when it was almost inevitable was in very greasy or rail conditions or if, on starting, the valves were in such a position that they were allowing only a very limited admission of steam to the cylinders. Unfortunately many drivers did not analyse what was happening and opened the regulator without due care, which resulted in the well-known slipping indicating their lack of artistry.

We stormed up Grosvenor bank with our train, crossed the Thames and very soon were passing over the top of the loco. We were gathering speed in the dark as we sped down the grade to Factory Junction, considerably faster than with any other engine I had been on. The way in which one was aware of the power of the locomotive and its mastery over the train remains with me still. I had put on the injector and opened the firedoors, the incandescent brilliance of the fire greeted me and I noted with some surprise the extent that the fire had dropped down from the lip of the firehole door. I placed half a dozen shovels round the back corners and under the door, steam held up well, 240 on breasting the climb to Clapham, but Hell! it was taking some coal! As fast as I shovelled it in, it seemed to disappear.

Steam was shut off after Clapham and, looking out again, even in the dark night I saw the darker black pall of coal smoke issue from the chimney, the acrid smell of it wafting onto the footplate. After Brixton, Two-Gun heaved the regulator open again and I then realised part of the reason at least for 34077's appetite was that he was working her quite heavily. We eased to take the curve through the north junction at Herne Hill and then started the climb proper. With a heavy thud that could be felt on the footplate of these engines when working really hard, we started climbing. As fast as I was feeding the insatiable box, so I saw fire shooting upwards, some bits so large they actually fell back and touched the casing before their red glow was lost. There was no chance of us sticking and we stormed over the top at about 30.

Soon we were at Eardley and our next two trips were also soon over, although they encompassed another two hours. The following trip was via Balham, a much less steeply graded route on which the engine was not worked as hard. On the final trip, the starter was on at Tulse Hill and we stopped in the station. A young porter, about my own age, looked in on us, marvelling at the fire as I opened the firedoors; Two-Gun remarked to him on the amount of coal I had been obliged to feed the brute. For my part I decided not to retort that some might not have been required had the regulator and reverser not been given such free reign! I did certainly wonder at the amount of coal consumed but my appetite had been whetted by the free and fast running of the class and I looked forward to some real main line work in the future on them.

Dobso and I still now and again teamed up but in the early winter I had another interesting turn with Two-Gun Smith. This was at dead of night, hauling a ten-coach load of empty stock from Clapham Junction to Lancing Works for overhaul. This was the only time I worked the whole way down the main line from London to Brighton, for of course all the passenger trains were electric and most of the goods work, so far as Stewarts Lane was concerned, ended at Three Bridges. Most of the through goods work anyway was from Norwood Junction, a good proportion of that being done by the Raworth/Bulleid Co-Co electric locos. Our engine was a U-boat, 31899, in fine fettle, so I enjoyed the run. Steam was coming in a-plenty and I always liked working up to the North Downs over the Quarry Line at night. The latter was built at the beginning of the century as an express avoiding line to the original one via Redhill to Brighton and had no stations on it. In consequence there was no attraction to build houses near it. As we entered the long chalk cutting that led to the Quarry Tunnel at the summit, it was as though one had cut off all contact with the rest of the world, no habitation or light being visible, while the chalk cliffs too looked a little unearthly.

We stopped at Three Bridges to take water. When we started away again, passing the busy goods yard, I enjoyed the combination that every fireman likes, although the engine was being worked hard, for about half a mile the safety valves were just lifted, giving a slight hiss indicating a nice hot fire along with a good steaming boiler. We got stopped by a signal at the end of Balcombe viaduct and, as I got on the phone to the signalman, one of the electric locos passed us with an up freight. They were looked down on by steam men but were rostered to do a prodigious amount of work per day, for if one failed it took about three steam engines to cover their duties. Inevitably they had a nick name – Hornbys. After Balcombe we had no further check but, just before we entered Patcham Tunnel, I looked out towards the village of that name, for ten years ,previously I had travelled this way, as a small schoolboy in an electric train to Brighton, to end up at Patcham as an evacuee from London at the outset of the Second World War. The rest of the trip was uneventful and we dropped our load of coaches at Lancing works; however, unbeknown to us, the real surprises of the trip were yet to come. We had to run light back to Brighton shed. It had been a cold night and now there were flurries of snow; as we sped tender-first towards our destination, we were becoming numbed with cold. Approaching Hove, Two-Gun shut the regulator and slowed the engine because something interesting was happening on the line from Brighton; a D3 tank engine had been in collision with a B1L electric train. The engine had merely its bogie derailed but the front of the electric was well and truly stoved in. The breakdown train was behind the electric, with its attendant staff busy putting matters to rights.

And so on to Brighton. Coming off the coast line, to get into the loco it is first necessary to run into Brighton station, then run back a few hundred yards into the loco, situated in the triangle of lines coming from the station. The fireman's position on the U-boats was on the left-hand side and, as we were tender-first, I was rather distant from the loco and was not too interested anyway, endeavouring as I was to get some circulation back into my body after our cold trip from Lancing. I was, in fact, busy gathering up the tools and loading them into the bucket preparatory to taking them back to the stores as we ran into the loco and it was only when we had stopped on the coal road and I straightened up to apply the handbrake that I became aware of a large locomotive a few roads away. A long grey body, turning up at the ends, with very large black painted bogies and big rectangular black boxes containing chain gear hanging on the outside of the bogies; a lazy wisp of grey smoke emanating from the roof at the near end. I gazed open-mouthed, as I saw in large white numerals on the side, 36001 – the prototype Leader class engine. The cab was locked and urged on by Two-Gun towards the station, for a London train was due to depart in ten minutes, I did not have time for further investigation. I believe, too, that later I imagined as more of the class came out I would be working on them. A wasted chance without doubt, for it was my first and last time of ever seeing the class. But for a combination of tiredness and cold, I am sure I would have stayed to have a more thorough investigation, although I was not to know that history decreed this was the only one to be completed and that after a few months of trials she would be withdrawn.

CHAPTER SIX

An interlude

Towards the end of 1949 I was booked on the night freight run to Three Bridges for the week with Harry Martin. This was the first time I had been booked for a whole week on such a turn, which was a fairly long goods run for the Southern, with usually a heavy load every night. It was the more interesting to me for we had three Q1 class goods engines for this type of duty; number 33036, 33039 and, the last one of the class, 33040. These engines were the most modern Southern Railway goods engines, having been built during the war. Due to the necessity for conserving materials, they had been built with just that object in mind and the result was widely thought by many to be the ugliest engine ever. Personally I have never subscribed to that, though I considered them to look the part that they were supposed to be, namely powerful, pugnacious, heavy freight engines. They had several unusual features. The boiler pressure, for instance, was 230 pounds per square inch; the valves like the preceding Q class, had outside admission valves and, like the Pacifics, they had five-nozzle Lemaitre exhausts. The firebox backplate and the tubeplate were the same as the Lord Nelson class but the footplate fittings were in the main different from the Nelsons, so that the similarity was not apparent. The driver's side of the footplate had a similar type of steam reverser to that fitted to the Q class and a long regulator handle was provided which made driving when seated a very comfortable job. The long handle was also continued on the fireman's side and could give much the same posterior tapping potential as that on the E2 tanks. Manipulation of the regulator was in fact easy, being the lightest balanced I ever operated. On the fireman's side, there was plenty of room, for the lubricators (unlike most Southern engines) were mechanical and mounted outside the cab. Both injectors were also on the fireman's side instead of the more usual arrangement of one each side of the footplate.

We departed from Battersea Yard at 10.50 p.m. and timing was fairly tight in the suburban area, for at that time of night there was still plenty of electric train traffic. The load was normally about 40 loaded wagons, and the route was via the Quarry line. The start gave the impression of the engine being master of the job, for it was a noticeably quick acceleration for so heavy a train. In addition, the exhaust from this class was absolutely distinctive, when working hard – not so much a blast as a shot! Quick sharp staccato barks when starting, however, gave way to a very soft exhaust when working at reduced cut-off at speed; we did have one regular turn to Eardley with coaching stock where over 50 m.p.h. was obtained and the class rode very well. At night, climbing up the grade between East Croydon and Coulsden North, the great network of roads with its thousands of houses on the western side of the line gave a beautiful mosaic of lights for miles into the distance; climbing up this section of the line was hard work, however, and the exhaust and its echo could be clearly heard in the silent night air but mostly I concentrated on steam pressure, for the demand was considerable. Although the boiler steamed well, I found it was best on them to fire little but often, ensuring a very white fire and making sure that the longish firebox didn't get much at the front, for the power and thrust from the wheels tended to cause the fire to run forward and, if choked at the front, steam very quickly became patchy.

After passing through Quarry Tunnel the line dropped for several miles towards Earlswood, just south of Redhill, where the line from London was again rejoined. Down the grade there was a chance to recoup a full head of steam and refill the boiler, and on the Q1s, as speed increased with the regulator shut, the rumble of the Bulleid-Firth Brown wheels became very audible from the footplate. This and the clanking of the coupling rods were both very distinctive signature tunes of the class.

Once through Earlswood steam was put on again, for this was the racing ground of the Brighton main line, with long straight undulating stretches, plus the pronounced dip at Horley station. Speed got quite high here even with a goods train, 45 m.p.h. being common. Just after Horley, one passed a little station, with prefabricated platforms on the local lines only. At this time of night it was closed – indeed at any time of the day it wore a permanent air of desertion. A little way away was a tiny club house and control tower, the only sign of habitation in view, dark and deserted at this hour, like the station. Peering in the gloom you might just make out the name on this strange structure – Gatwick Airport.

Not long after passing there, the regulator was shut as we neared our destination, speed steadily dropped and, as we entered Three Bridges station, the regulator was again opened to haul our train slowly into the yard. We arrived about 12.30 and, after unhooking, had to wait for the last train of the night from Victoria to Brighton to hurtle through. This comprised two 6-PUL units of ten green coaches and two Pullmans, doing about 70 m.p.h. We could then cross the main to the up side to run up to the neck and then reverse back to enter Three Bridges loco. Later, as I shall relate, I often worked to Three Bridges and back with other locomotives a few years later, but by that time all the Q1 class had been drafted away to other sheds.

My first rostered position in the Herne Hill link meant, in fact, that I did not serve in the lowest link of all at the depot, which consisted of very local shunting turns. One of these was of some interest, however, and early in 1950 I did have to cover it on a couple of days. This was the C.W.S. milk pilot duty. The Co-op depot at Stewarts Lane lay between the large carriage shed, situated about a hundred yards to the west of the loco, and the back of Longhedge works. The rail entry to it was on an extremely tight curve, so that only engines with less than an 11′ coupled wheel-base were allowed to enter – anything bigger being bound to become derailed. For many years the old 1302 class crane tank had been retained for use on this duty – hence it survived so long. By the mid-1940s, however, it was feeling the effects of old age and something else had to be found. In 1945, therefore, the old Southampton Docks Company 0–4–0ST 3458 *Ironside* was sent to Stewarts Lane from Guildford shed, where it had resided for years. It was to take over 1302's job whilst the latter went to Ashford for an intermediate overhaul. 3458 stayed some months, then returned to its old haunts when 1302 returned. The C.W.S. hired both the engine and crew, so there were great pains taken always to see an engine and crew were provided, because, if not available, valuable revenue would be lost. The problem was that 1302 had no standby and when required to be washed out every couple of weeks, a rush job had to be made of it to get her back to the milk depot on time. Early in 1948, this problem was solved by transferring B4 dock engine 88 to Stewarts Lane, as the USA tanks had taken the B4s place at Southampton. From then on 88 became the regular engine; until its eventual demise 1302 was only lit up once every couple of weeks for one day's work whilst 88 had a washout. I never fired 88 but did take a trip on her with Harry Ward after leaving the Herne Hill link. She ran quite steadily, with a good turn of speed for a small-wheel 0-4-0 tank and steamed freely, being much more popular than her predecessor. Towards the end of 1949, she went elsewhere and another named engine came to replace her. Before that happened, however, I was on a Preparation and disposal turn (P & D for short) and was deputed on my own to thrown the fire out of old 1302 after her fortnightly stint. She had a minute clinker shovel for this purpose, smaller in breadth than a firing shovel and I celebrated the occasion after completing the job by helping to reduce her steam pressure with a few toots on her whistle; this at least was life size!

The replacement was as obscure an engine as old *Ironside* but from much further west, No. 756 *A.S. Harris*, which originated from the Hawthorn Leslie company in 1907, being built for the Plymouth, Devonport & South West Junction Railway. It was an outside cylinder six-coupled tank engine, with a

Belpaire firebox and had obviously seen better days by the time we got it. Surmounting her chimney was a copper cap and, as time went by, small holes appeared towards the base of the chimney, through which wisps of smoke made their way. One fateful day, when she started snorting out of the milk dock working a bit hard, the blast shot the copper cap feet into the air as it parted company with the base and clattered to the ground. 1302 took over for a few days and the shed staff fashioned a tube, which they fitted into the remaining sound piece attached to the smokebox and then refixed the cap. This improvisation lasted for another eighteen months until the engine was withdrawn. Early in 1950 I found myself booked for the turn. 756 was the engine and for an hour or so while stationary in the milk dock the engine steamed very well. At length, with the couple of milk tanks emptied, we had to shunt them to the goods yard to pick up another pair to replace them. Virtually as soon as the regulator was opened, pressure started to drop; the first port of the regulator seemed to do no more than tighten the couplings so that it required the second port, which fairly depleted the meagre boiler resources. With pressure down from 170 to 130 in not time, the vacuum train pipe pressure started to drop an inch or two and the brakes started to rub gently. After a couple of shunts, then back to the dock (placing the tanks again for emptying) pressure was down to 120 and about a third of the boiler gauge had water, indicating quite a thirsty engine. We had now about another hour before anything active needed to be done again, so it was time to put on the injector to refill the boiler. It made a lot of noise sucking in air and the amount of water being injected into the boiler was minimal; it took over a quarter of an hour before the task was accomplished. It was the same performance every shunt, so that what should have been a simple job became rather a task with the poor old tool provided. Shortly afterwards, however, rescue came in the form of the final motive power provided for this job. Three S.E.C.R. P class six-coupled tanks arrived (31555, 31557 and 1558), which proved to be ideal and after a short period 756 and 1302 were pensioned off.

Reverting to 756, however, to one of the staff at Stewarts Lane she was no stranger. We had a few enginemen hailing from the West Country and one of them had been a fireman on the P.D.S.W.J.R. in 1910 and fired 756 in her original blue livery all those years ago. Yarns of daily doings were, and no doubt still are, one of the great interests between footplatemen and I have heard many swapped. The last journey of 1302 was one of these. The old Crane tank was past any pretence of speed, if indeed she had ever had any, and therefore she was booked to depart to Ashford at dead of night, when line occupation was at its minimum and she would not inconvenience anyone. Having no power brakes at the end, and a very limited water capacity, a number of stops were required en route both to take water and to fire her, for there was little room on her footplate for any activity except standing. So she waddled off on her final argosy, being booked to run via the Maidstone West line, in order to keep her off the main routes as much as possible. She was supposed to arrive at Ashford at about 6 o'clock in the morning but things did not go well. The pace proved much too hectic and so it was not until 7 o'clock that she lurched into Maidstone to take water. The commuters waiting for the London train on the opposite platform lowered their newspapers and I was assured by the unfortunate fireman on board that all broke into spontaneous laughter at the sight of the old relic. I had a soft spot for her, regardless.

For many years there had been no really old representatives of the former L.B.S.C.R. but to my delight early in 1950 there was transferred to the shed a real veteran, 32128, a Stroudley E1 goods tank, built at Brighton works in 1878 (and when new named *Avignon)*. She was much as when originally constructed, except that she had been fitted with a Drummond chimney.

Towards mid March my turn came with her. Dobso and I were booked together for a week on 67 duty, the old Herne Hill link Departmental turn to Battersea yard. The footplate was plain and simple, with everything just where it should be. The only new thing to me was the air brake handle, which was mounted vertically and moved round a semi-circular guide. The reverse was by lever. We were pointing engine-first towards Battersea Yard, which suited me very well, for I was positioned on the shunter's side and had to interpret his signals. It was found to be best if I opened and shut the regulator, shouting to Dobso on the other side when to apply the brake or when to throw the reversing lever. One morning when I arrived for work before Dobso, the foreman gave me a choice of engines – an H class or the E1. I plumped for the latter, for there were not many chances of working on Stroudley engines. Dobso discovered my choice just before we were about to start work. "You should have had the H", he said. "Much easier to work!" This was the truth, for the driving, braking and reversing could all be done by the same man. "I'd have let you do the driving", he concluded. He did not understand; it was no use explaining.

On the penultimate day on this turn we nearly shut the shed down with 32128. Our last bit of work was to bring the locomotive coal back to Stewarts Lane goods yard and on this particular day there was an abnormally heavy load. The shunter asked my mate if he was prepared to take all 30 wagons, which was an overload for the class and he agreed. When we started away the Ramsbottom safety valves were humming away nicely with pressure at 160 pounds but getting this load on the move, however, did require quite an effort, particularly as we snaked over the crossings that approached Stewarts Lane. The entrance to the Yard was through the carriage washing plant; as we approached the latter, we saw the shunter some way ahead in the yard signal us to stop, for quite often a lot of shunting, with the Yard pilot, the milk pilot or light engines to and from the sheds, took place. A fairly heavy application was needed to hold the heavy load behind us and we came to a halt with just the chimney standing in the washing machine, for we were working bunker-first. The long train trailed out behind us and blocked all the roads into and out of the loco. We were not unduly perturbed, for it was quite usual to be held here for about a minute. I had the injector on because we had used quite a bit of water pressure having dropped to about 130. Sure enough, after about a minute the shunter signalled us to pull up. The regulator was opened, the couplings progressively tightened down our long line of wagons and then the wheels slipped. We were not moving the train. We had been standing where water in gallons cascades from the wash and the rails were thoroughly wet and greasy. Easing the engine back to the train and then trying a couple of times again proved no more successful. Then we became aware that the West Country for 'The Golden Arrow' was waiting to leave the loco. At the same moment I saw Algy Hiss, the foreman, with red and agitated countenance making a hasty way towards us from his office. I shut the injector off and quickly stirred the fire with the pricker, then gathered some sand from the sandbox onto my shovel. Running alongside the engine, I thrust it under the wheels on both sides. Dobso waited for a few more seconds for pressure to rise, then tried again. A half slip, silence, the engine moving just perceptively backwards, an enormous 'woof' as the valve opened to exhaust, another painful silence, and another 'woof'. We were now not slipping and must have been doing all of 2 m.p.h. Gradually, gradually, the exhaust came a bit more frequently and, after another half a minute, we knew we were going to win. A couple of minutes later and the Arrow engine was on its way. I fired 32128 once more; this was on 31st March 1950 when, with driver Dishman, I worked her on shed shunting duties, hauling dead engines round as required to various roads in the depot. It was, in fact, my last day of footplate work for over two years, for on 5th April I was due to join the Army for National service. On that last day one of the most shapely of engines was in the shed as a visitor, J1 tank 32325 of Tunbridge Wells, painted in malachite green without any designation of ownership on her tanks. She too would be a thing of the past when I got back.

On 13th April 1950 I travelled by train from Kings Cross to Darlington, hauled by A3 60081 *Shotover,* as a reluctant conscript in His Majesty's Army. The outbreak of the Korean War extended National Service to two years. It was therefore not until April 1952 that I arrived back in civilian life. On 15th January 1952, whilst on leave, I had visited Stewarts Lane to look up old friends; my next visit was back in overalls when I returned in earnest on 7th May 1952.

CHAPTER SEVEN

Many Happy Returns

During and after the war, many locomotives which should have been withdrawn had to be patched up to keep going for a further period. On the Southern, new production for the years 1946 to 1949 was exclusively main line express types. The result was that elderly engines had to soldier on, urgent attention having to be given to their replacement once the railways had been Nationalised. Overdue was the replacement of engines that were working the secondary steam services to London from Sussex, from Lewes, Tunbridge Wells, and the East Grinstead areas. In the main these were worked by the I3, E4, E5, D3, and the J1 and J2 tanks of the L.B.S.C.R. In 1950 Brighton works was given orders to build 41 L.M.S. type 2-6-4 tanks to replace them, numbered 42066 to 42106. In addition, some 2-6-2 tank engines, built at Crewe in 1951-52 and numbered 41290 upwards, were allocated to the Southern. When I returned, the I3 and the J tanks had been eliminated, along with my old friends the H1 Atlantics; the E5 and D3s were also well on the way out. The South Eastern & Chatham classes, however, had been virtually unaffected, except that considerable inroads had been made into the R and R1 0-4-4 tanks and, as a result, a number of the H class had been fitted for motor working to be used as replacements for them.

There were interesting changes as well at the other end of the scale. The Night Ferry train with its heavy Continental sleeping cars was originally hauled by a light Pacific but it had proved to be such a weighty proposition (and water consumption had been heavy, requiring an extra stop at times) that soon after its introduction the train became double-headed, with provision of an additional engine in the shape of an L1 4-4-0. Double-heading was rarely allowed on the Southern, being prohibited on certain tightly-curved routes because of the possibility of buffer locking and eventually an alternative solution was provided. This was done by transferring Merchant Navy Pacifics 35026 – 35030 to the Eastern Section, where they were shared between Stewarts Lane and Dover depots and almost exclusively employed on the Boat trains. In addition, 'The Golden Arrow' had been hauled by light Pacifics for several years but such a prestige train was apparently too tempting a morsel for the Railway Executive and in 1951 two Standard Britannia Pacifics had been transferred to Stewarts Lane to work it. The locomotive usually employed on the train had, in fact, for some months in 1951 been stationed a few miles from Stewarts Lane but not on the Region. This was 70004 *William Shakespeare,* which stood as an exhibit in the Festival of Britain exhibition; the other was 70014 *Iron Duke,* which relieved from time to time but was also employed on other boat train duties.

This then was the scene when I returned and I looked forward to reacquaintance with the old and to meeting the new.

My first day was something of a holiday. I booked on at the gentlemanly hour of eight in the morning, as a spare man, with Sid King, who must have qualified as one of the world's worst worriers. Old Sid was a man with a kindly enough nature, but suffered plenty of leg-pulling from his collegues, for he took most things literally and believed most that he was told. Consequently he was fed the most unlikely stories, so that his mates could watch the credulous reaction which this produced, although I have a sneaking suspicion that he played up to them at times and had a secret laugh at their expense. Certainly he was not one of the world's greatest enginemen for, although a willing worker, he had little of the instinctive feel for the job which was essential. The favourite story about him was one concerning the Norwood Goods. He was driving a return working from Norwood with a W class and, after passing through Balham, then accelerating down the grade towards Clapham Junction a couple of miles distant, he made a full application of the powerful steam brake. He then remarked to his mate how quietly the engine ran and how he could not even hear the rail joints. That should have told him something, but alas it didn't and he left the brake applied until after the grade flattened out after passing through the Junction. When he released the brake, there was an almighty bang as the wheels started to rotate again, having been locked solid for the past couple of miles, which had resulted in enormous flats on the drivers and caused him to end up on the carpet to account for the necessity to retyre all the driving wheels.

There was very little to do the first day and we only got one job, to dispose one of the new 2-6-4 tanks, No.42105. I found this of interest, however, for it illustrated how the Southern Railway had fallen behind in labour saving respects when compared with other railways. The self-cleaning smokebox, drop grate and ash pan cleared by operating a lever situated just above rail level were a revelation and a far cry from the pre-Bulleid engines – which involved shovelling everything from everywhere. I was later to find that my high regard for the 4MT tanks on the shed was to be somewhat moderated by their performance on the road.

The next day was one for old friends, for I was back on E2 tank 32103 on the Herne Hill pilot and Clapham Goods turn but these first couple of days were just make-weights until I could be fitted into the programme for training fireman which had been incorporated whilst I had been away. In the intervening period, recruitment of footplate staff had become difficult, as there were more attractive jobs elsewhere which gave equal or better renumeration without the inconvenient hours or the necessity to work at weekends. This had resulted in a shortage of firemen and promotion had quickened, sometimes putting inexperienced fireman on quite demanding jobs and had resulted in decreasing standards of timekeeping. As a result, all passed cleaners before being appointed had to attend a firing school set up at Bricklayers Arms shed. This had consisted of a week of lectures, films and then third man attachments. It had also been decided that all returning servicemen should attend this course. Personally, I thought that a couple of years' previous footplate experience made the whole thing a little unnecessary as far as I was concerned. None the less, on 9th May I booked on at 7.55 a.m. as third man on No.13 duty, which involved working the 8.35 a.m. to Ramsgate and the 1.10 p.m. from there to Victoria. The engine had been prepared for us, and on this first day it was King Arthur 30794 *Sir Ector De Maris,* a regular Stewarts Lane small-tender version of the class. Most of them sported 8-wheel tenders of 5,000 gallons capacity but 30793–30806 had been built in 1926/7 with shorter 6-wheel tenders for use on the Brighton main line. These carried 3,500 gallons but were capable of being turned on the shorter turntables at the former Brighton sheds. With the Brighton Line electrification of 1933 they had been transferred to Eastern section sheds.

I had worked on the Arthurs only on turns to and from Victoria or empty stock duties up to now but at least I was thoroughly familiar with their footplates. The layout was of L.S.W.R. origin, the large centrally-positioned regulator handle being a typical Drummond design, having a big oval-patterned head, with a long tapered arm extending about three feet to the working end. This had a rounded shank which fitted nicely into the hand and, when pushed away, opened or, when pulled, shut. It was a balanced regulator, very positive to use and always stayed in the position placed, unlike some which, with vibration, became self-shutting. The only disadvantage it had was that it was necessary to come from observation of the road for an instant to close it. It was usual to leave the regulator open on the main port when driving and adjust power by use of the reverser. This was a heavy, wheel-operated piece of equipment; however, it could be dexterously operated by acquiring a knack of twists of the wrists, which moved it to the required position reasonably easily and a large sector plate mounted on top of the reverser enabled the cut-off to be readily seen. The firehole door was another Drummond feature, worked by a rachet-mounted handle. When this pointed to the cab roof the firehole, which consisted of a metal flap, was

2-6-2T No. 41293 at Longhedge Junction, with the author looking out of the side window — a photograph taken shortly after the collision with the King Arthur as related on pages 89-90. The coal elevator at Stewarts Lane is in the background. [Photo: K.G. Carr]

A rather faded photograph of the author in army uniform on the footplate of No. 35026 **Lamport & Holt Line** *at Stewarts Lane shed, 5 January 1952.*

completely closed. To open it, the handle was moved down to the horizontal and the door, being hinged, moved from vertically down to horizontally up, poking forward inside the firebox. It was a simple but good design, for not only was it quick and easy to operate but it channelled the cold air into the heart of the fire, giving it a chance to heat before coming into contact with the tubeplate.

One of the paradoxes of footplate work was to find out how different engines looked from the footplate compared with the more familiar view from the lineside. The Arthurs were a fairly typically proportioned Edwardian express engine, with a very slightly tapered boiler. From the footplate looking forward through the large kidney-shaped windows, the surprising feature was that the slight taper was accentuated by the length of the boiler barrel and there was an impression of a towering footplate sharply tapering to the smokebox, where the chimney stood high and clear in the wild blue yonder. Observation through the spectacle plates was good, except that it was somewhat restricted straight ahead due to the bulk of the smokebox and protruding smoke deflectors.

Such then was the footplate that I was mounted on for my first trip to the Kent Coast, as Bill Jones put the regulator full over and we moved the 8.35 away from Victoria. I always recall the reputed remarks of a French locomotive engineer on first experience of the class "Mon Dieu, but how she shouts!" And indeed they all did when starting away, as it was generally a case of full regulator and full forward gear for the first couple of hundred yards. The exhaust was like gunfire, which could be felt as well as heard, for the Arthurs were very good at keeping their feet, being only prone to slipping on the most greasy of rails. Once on the move, the reverser would be wound back and the exhaust quietened to a respectable level. I sat on the lid of the long wood clothing box – which was not used overmuch once business had started in earnest. I forget who the fireman was but the general plan was that I was to observe him for a bit and then try my hand at proceedings. The engine was worked hard up to Grosvenor Bridge spanning the Thames and then speed started to increase.

Firing had been in the classic tradition of little and often, with big shovelfuls deposited under the door and back corners, a couple along the sides of the box plus, now and again, a couple of lightly loaded shovels to the front end of the box. To do this was almost a theatrical performance; with the shovel only lightly loaded, it was inclined back towards the tender pointing at about 30° to the floor, and then with a quick, quarter-circular motion propelled forward until the blade just entered the firebox and then stopped. The contents would then shoot the nine feet to the front. With experience, it was surprising how accurate delivery could be, bearing in mind that all the time the footplate was moving forward, sideways, up or down in varying degrees. I noted too that from my perch I could see what was going on on the footplate and then stick my head out the side of the cab, and in doing so saw that, as soon as each shovelful was delivered into the box, a short puff of black smoke emerged from the chimney, a sure sign of a high firebox temperature, and consequently a good steaming boiler. I was also getting accustomed to the motion of the class at speed. They rode solidly, as solid as they looked, for indeed they were heaviest two-cylinder express engine in the kingdom. Once into the 65 to 70 m.p.h. range they could not be pushed to any higher speed, although they could always be relied upon to tackle heavy loads. They were felt to be a reliable engine but rather bland in performance – not a bad thing for the average crew who wanted an engine that would get them there without problems of steaming or running, even if they did not set the Thames on fire in doing so. Bad rail joints on crossings they could pick out, for they ran, to my mind, as though the driving wheels were anchored to the running rails and laid the tracks flat – but they could give a kick on the footplate quite unexpectedly if a poor joint was encountered. So, noting what was going on, we had arrived at Bromley South, our first stop.

"How did I feel about doing some work?" the fireman enquired. I was ready, willing and able, so we exchanged places. The pressure was just on the 200 pound mark, with a quiet drift of steam from the safety valves. The boiler was full, so for the moment my services were superfluous. We started away, shouting our way up Bromley bank to Bickley and I noted with satisfaction the rapid way the fire changed from deep gold to near white flame. Before I started firing, I had a look into the box to see how the fire was bedded. This was done by putting the blade of the shovel into the firehole door which directed a path of air along it onto the burning coal; by moving the shovel about, one had an accurate picture of how the fire lay and could see if there were any deficiencies or any places where it was too thick. All that could be seen otherwise was a mass of incandescent flame which obscured the true state of the firebox contents, except for the area immediately in the vicinity of the firehole door.

We had departed from Bromley South at 8.56 and our next stop was Chatham, 23½ miles distant, which was booked to be covered at an average speed of 43 m.p.h. Once the climb to Bickley had been made, we had fourteen miles of undulating track to the top of Sole Street bank, the most advantageous stretch being the descent to Farningham Road. I copied the method adopted by the fireman of little and often, finding a bit of difficulty in keeping my feet firmly placed when making the longer shots down the length of the box. Just before Bickley I had put on the injector. On the Arthurs, the one on the fireman's side was an exhaust steam injector, which had the economy virtue of utilising some of the exhaust steam to work it. The valve for this part of the injector was mounted just to the left and in front of the fireman's window, from whence a rod passed through the cab front into the cab and was operated by a wheel some 6″ in diameter. Once the water handle had been opened on the tender, this handle was opened to allow the exhaust steam to work the injector but, in addition, to initially open the injector clack and to work the injector when the regulator was shut, another live steam valve had to be opened. This was positioned on the centre of the boiler back and I found I had almost to go on tiptoe to operate these handles. I found a careful eye had to be kept on the injector feed when the regulator was shut, for the changeover from exhaust to live steam was achieved by an automatic valve within the injector control mechanism but, if the live steam valve had not been opened quite sufficiently, the injector would stop feeding the boiler and the water feed would be running away through the overflow pipe onto the track. On the other hand, if too much live steam was being admitted, it could cause the injector to fly off, with a stream of water being carried along on the powerful jet of steam roaring out of the overflow pipe.

We galloped through Farningham Road at about 70 and then steadied to a fast but gradually slowing climb up to Fawkham. Then on to Longfield, a climb of some four miles, the last mile or so at 1 in 100, which made working somewhat harder. I found I was maintaining pressure at about 175 pounds, the aim on this class being usually about 180 at least, so that I was just below par. Using the shovel to look into the fire, I found that some of my long throws had been high and had hit the brick arch, building a haycock below it to one side. Heaving the 11′ long pricker from the tender was not a recommended exercise and required careful planning so as not to hit any passing bridge or train, but I had to do so to level the fire towards the front. I then had to return it to the tender again. Back to firing, I found I was getting into a rhythm; snap open the door, with the shovel already loaded, swing, back left corner, back right corner, under the door, along one side, along the other side, snap the door closed, then a quick glance at the chimney to observe the fading smoke. At length we reached the summit of the climb out of London at Sole Street and began the descent of the bank that I had last clanked down in the old WD 2-8-0 nearly three years before. This time we were going over the top much faster as I moved over to the fireman's side and held fast to the handrail to the rear of the side sheet lookout. We raced down the bank, which is mostly at 1 in a 100 for five miles and, after some three miles, were approaching the 80 m.p.h. mark. Even *Sir Ector* began to get somewhat lively and less anchored to the rails. This was new to me. The noise, speed and pitching were admittedly just a little anxiety-creating, particularly as after Cuxton Road box the line took a distinctly sharp curve to the right. Would our speed be reduced enough to stop us shooting off the curve? The answer was not long in coming for Bill Jones gently but firmly brought back the brake handle and the familiar hiss of air entering the holes on the handle and into the train pipe could be heard above the general din. The rumble and roar of the train took on a different note as the brakes bit and it was surprising how rapidly the speed fell away. We passed the well known outline of Cuxton Road at about 40, gathering a little pace after we rounded the curve and train pipe pressure gradually mounted up to the full release pressure of 21 inches. We next trundled across the Medway, put steam on to pass through Rochester station with its long platform, then into the short tunnel and so into Chatham station, deep in its black, brick-lined cutting.

Full boiler pressure and full boiler, such was now the happy state of affairs. The crew had been content enough with my performance, so I was left to fire the engine for the rest of the journey. Chatham station in its cavern was an ideal sounding board to reflect the shout of our 4-6-0 starting away into the tunnel and up the stiff climb up to Gillingham, the next stop only a couple of miles away. After a brief stop there, it was a fast run through the undulating Kent countryside, stopping at Sittingbourne and Faversham.

Departing from the latter, we were now on ground new to me. We diverged from the line to Canterbury and Dover and turned towards the North Kent coast, passing the small shed at Faversham between the Dover and Ramsgate lines. The line ahead lay flat and straight so, with the engine worked fairly easily, we were soon running into the sixties, with pressure easily maintained at about 185 pounds. I had time to look around and enjoy the scenery; the line passed through the Graveney marshes, on an embankment about 10′ above them, this part of the country being very sparsely inhabited due to the nature of the ground, although the undulating meadows were very lush. At last the sea side, with small coves and, here and there, family parties on the patches of beach, as at Seasalter. A couple of minutes later the regulator was shut and we coasted to a halt at the first of the Kent Coast resorts, Whitstable.

Station stops on the Southern were always tightly timed, so that within a minute we were on our way again, this time climbing away to pass under the overline bridge of the oldest railway in Kent, the Canterbury & Whitstable line. At this time, this was still open for goods traffic and, on account of the small bore of Tyler Hill tunnel, was worked exclusively by the cut-down version of the Stirling R1 six-coupled tanks. No sooner did we start moving at a respectable speed than we were running into Herne Bay. Another short stop then away again, this time for a quarter of an hour's uninterrupted run to Birchington. From there although there are stations every couple of miles, the boarding houses, hotels, and other habitations form one continuous line, so that this first sight of Birchington, Westgate and Margate was one confusing whole and I was unable to deduce where one town ended and the other began. When we came to a halt at Margate, I found that the station – which was the biggest by far of those we had called at – was only a hundred yards from the sea, the entertainment facilities and esplanade being clearly visible from the footplate, which was a refreshing sight to my now slightly flagging spirits.

So we started away on our last lap, climbing the straight and steady gradient from Margate, the line having turned inland immediately after the station towards the open country. Halfway up the bank and before we again got to the rural area, lay the most peculiar station I ever came across. At a point which looked no different from the rest of the permanent way, were two boards, one each side of the line which in faded characters proclaimed this to be MARGATE EAST. The only facility provided was a flight of steps each side of the line to enable passengers to get to rail level. They were accompanied by the sole member of staff – who was booking clerk and ticket collector. From the passengers' point of view he had also the most important task of providing the means for them to board or alight from the trains. This was a ladder-like conveyance on wheels which he trundled to the nearest carriage door. Fortunately, traffic was very light and I believe the station was only provided for the residential district of Cliftonville, only a limited number of trains per day calling.

For a few minutes we now ran into open country and the fireman advised me to let the fire run down. But as steam demand was still considerable, it was necessary to push the fire over to a more even depth to prevent any dead patches developing. So we ran into Broadstairs and again a more or less unbroken conurbation commenced. We started away and immediately hit the steepish bank that led nearly all the way up to Ramsgate station; topping the rise we ran into our destination, with the loco on our right and the carriage sheds just beyond. On the whole I considered it had been a very easy run. I had fired some 70 miles, with pressure maintained well all the way. It had been hard work but I took pride in that I had managed it, and the regular fireman had not had to take the shovel away from me. With experience it would no doubt be easier; as it was, I judged the King Arthurs to be friendly old engines without vices. I was to find in the fullness of time it usually was not quite so simple but that was for the future.

The shunter unhooked us from the train and we trundled off to Ramsgate loco. The front of the tender was now almost bare of coal, so on shed the fireman asked me to shovel some forward from the back of the tender, while he set about clearing the worst of the clinker from the fire for the return journey.

Shovelling the coal forward was done in order to build up the fire ready for our return journey, for Stewarts Lane was provided with Nottinghamshire coal which, although larger, was in appearance and effect very like domestic coal and burnt readily, emitting fairly black smoke. We were about to take on the local Kent coal which I had not come across before but apparently it took some time to ignite and produce heat enough for steam production. This could be aided, however, if it was fed onto a bed of quick burning Nottinghamshire coal. When we had built up the fire with the damper only just open and the blower only just carrying the smoke lightly up the chimney, we backed under the coal hopper and took on a supply of Kent coal. I examined it with considerable interest for it was unlike any I had come across before. There were no veins in it like Nottingham coal and, instead of the slab-like appearance I was used to, most of it was of large irregularly shaped lumps, not black in colour but very light grey, glittering with innumerable tiny silver crystals. Small pieces could be broken off in the hand and it then crumbled easily. If Nottingham coal was hit with the hammer, it gave a loud crack when contact was made, splinters from the surface flying off in all directions. This coal when hit, however, emitted a muffled hollow clonk and readily broke into pieces. The relative weight was also of interest, the Kent variety being much heavier for the same mass.

Once the worst of the dirt had been cleaned from the fire, having assisted in building it up again, I went under the engine and cleaned the ashpan. We next took water and turned the engine. Then, having had a well-deserved and much needed wash, we had time to get something to eat and brew a can of tea. After this repast, I decided I had a little time to look round the depot before we had to mount 30794 for our return journey.

Ramsgate was a moderately-sized loco with an allocation of engines somewhat similar to that at our own depot, namely a mix of S.E.C.R. and Southern engines but I came across one unusual and real veteran. There was an old engine, painted grey, standing on some buffer stops on a dead end, with permanent pipe connections which proclaimed that it had been used as a hot water boiler for many a year. Getting closer, I was amazed to see that it was a domeless Stirling engine, with the safety valves bang in the middle of the boiler where the dome was usually located. The crank axle was missing and the tender was one of the old outside frame variety with the springs outside above the frame. There was no identity but it retained the original chimney and I recognised it as an original unrebuilt O class of the South Eastern Railway. Subsequently, I was to learn that this was No.98, withdrawn from service in 1929 after thirty years' service and employed until 1953 as a hot water boiler, when it was replaced by D class 31501 and scrapped. It was the last domeless engine to remain in use, not only on the Southern but in the country.

Having had a swift Cook's tour, we boarded our faithful steed for the return journey. It had been decided that I would be given a rest now and could instead study the effects of firing with Kent coal, but I was also keen to tackle the formidable climb up Sole Street bank, so I was to take over the responsibility for firing again when we arrived at Gillingham.

At 1.10, with myself once more seated on the fireman's side, we set out for Victoria, regulator open just on the second port, safety valves open, for pressure stood at 200 pounds; we started down the grade towards Dumpton Park.

In the early years of the century the D class 4-4-0s had been introduced as the principal express engines of the S.E.C.R. After running for a short time, trouble was experienced with leaking tubes and excessive priming. This was largely found to be caused by the very hard Kentish water and steps were taken to treat it to overcome these problems. Although a considerable improvement was made, even to the end of steam operation, Kent water was still inferior to that from other parts of the region and still caused a certain amount of trouble.

This I now found out for, although we were on an easy grade, the chemical action of the water became apparent. Foaming water as well as steam passed down the main steam pipe and into the cylinders, while a mixture of the same started to gush upwards from the chimney, a classic case of priming. The effects were very pronounced, for instead of the loud bark of the exhaust we heard a muffled, almost continual and subdued woosh. It is essential in such circumstances to relieve the pressure in the cylinders, so the cylinder cocks must be opened at once to allow water lying in the cylinders and not carried up to the blast pipe to escape. When this is done, the view forward disappears in clouds of steam and moisture, while power drops off both because of the inefficiency of the steam/water mixture, and the release of pressure due to the opening of the cylinder cocks. Incidentally, hydraulic pressure is such that I

No. 31145, a D1 class Superheater, carrying a 74c Dover shedplate, standing on No. 19 road in the sandhole at Stewarts Lane, June 1953. The bridge visible in the background is the Kent Coast main line. **Below:** *King Arthur No. 30763* **Sir Bors de Ganis** *in typically well-cleaned condition. She is standing on 17 road with the main shed and roads 1-16 behind; June 1953.*

30918 **Hurstpierpoint** *was one of the various Schools class that I fired during my career; they were excellent engines apart from being somewhat prone to losing their feet.*

once saw the cylinder head blown off an N class 2-6-0 in these circumstances – not, I am glad to say, on my engine. The King Arthurs seemed to be the worst engines affected by Kentish water and it was an expected, indeed to some extent welcomed, reaction when starting away from Ramsgate, for once the worst of the salts had primed away down to Dumpton Park, unless the boiler had not been washed out for some time, it did not seem to reoccur on the journey. Moreover, the favourable grade enabled pressure and water to be easily regained before any heavy work was required. The Arthurs had long, tall, water gauges and the other effect very noticeable was the dropping of the water level in the glass, with a browny-grey head of foam sitting on top of the water. It would have done credit to any pint of mild and bitter. After about thirty seconds, the priming died away, the regulator was shut and we drifted down to the station, whilst the injector was put on to recoup the water lost.

Our load outward had been ten coaches but on this mid-afternoon return we started out with only six. At Faversham we picked up a further four, which were shunted onto us by the station pilot, these four coaches forming a through train from Dover which had stopped at all stations and arrived at Faversham nine minutes before us.

We arrived at Gillingham at 2.45 p.m., running in past the small shed on the country side of the station, which at this period had mostly H,C, and D class engines. My tutor had handed me over a really hot fire and full head of steam and water. We ran down the hill to Chatham, where we took water and, having a three minute stand, the safety valves were roaring away before the regulator was opened for the climb up to Sole Street.

Speed rose to about 30 m.p.h. as we crossed the Medway for the second time, but the regulator was then closed, for the acute curve at the bottom of the bank had a 25 m.p.h. restriction, so no run was possible, and it was slog all the way. One of the silly rivalries of the South Eastern and London Chatham & Dover companies was apparent as we crossed the river, for each railway could not abide the other, so they both had to build their own bridges over the river. Once the amalgamation took place, the S.E.R. bridge became redundant but it was there still, empty, useless and still a liability, in that it had to be kept in a safe condition.

I had left the injector on until the regulator was opened for the climb, so that with a full boiler I could have as much steam available for the initial part of the climb. We accelerated to about 35 and the regulator was left with full second port open. Cut-off was about 40 to 45 per cent, power being regulated up the bank only by variation of the cut-off. The fireman was, in fact, on this stretch on a hiding to nothing. If speed dropped off, the cut-off was advanced to work the engine harder. If speed increased, and this was only by a few m.p.h., again cut-off was advanced to climb quicker, so the solution was keep pressure up as high as possible. Such heavy working took rapid toll of water level, so in fact once the injector was put on again it had to be forgotten, as level was bound to drop. The only exception was that if steaming was poor it might be necessary to hold the position to turn it off for a short time to conserve steam but this was a last resort.

So 30794 started to slog, exhaust sharp, not over quick, with a pronounced sway on the footplate to one side or the other as power was transmitted through the big ends on each side. I found firing little and often, keeping a very hot fire, was the thing and I now saw the extraordinary difference Kent coal made when really hot. Like Topsy it just growed and growed and growed, for as it heated right through it swelled like a great and grotesque sponge, occupying about four times the space of its former natural size. On firing there was just the faintest darkening of the exhaust, not the pronounced blackness of Nottinghamshire coal. Mile after mile of 1 in 100, with the line gradually turning as we ascended and far below to our right the line from Strood to Maidstone could be seen wending its way along the Medway Valley. *Sir Ector* chonked on, the beat very regular and steam was holding up well between 175 and 180 but the water level was starting to creep down from the top of the glass. Not so good, for with the engine going uphill, the water was higher at the firebox end than the smokebox end of the boiler, which meant that when the summit was reached the level in the glass would drop a fair bit. Then perceptively speed started to increase without any change in the cut-off. This indicated we were about half a mile from the top, as the gradient reduced to 1 in 350 towards the top. Seconds later, Sole Street station hove into sight and we went over the top accelerating rapidly as we dropped down towards Meopham station a couple of miles distant. Sure enough, the water fell rapidly down the glass until it levelled out just below the half way mark; with the lighter working, however, a slow recovery of the level could be expected. Gradually speed was being worked up without pushing the engine unduly and soon we were shooting through Farningham Road at about 70. In no time at all we were running into Bromley South, our last stop. When we came to a stand I noted the water was now bobbing in the top of the glass and so shut off the injector. "Victoria only" intoned the station announcer, so in 20 minutes we would have completed our run. The engine, after all this fast and heavy work, was hot; there was a combination of sights and smells I was to get used to in the future which I was now getting to know for the first time. The hot oily smell from the cylinders, a steely hot smell from the brakes and the faint haze and heat coming up from the ashpan below, which had a fair quantity of hot ash wafting up a faint blue smoke.

Once more the exhaust shouted as we started down the grade from Bromley. Not much more work now. A bit of firing under the door, for steam had to be kept well up to ascend to Penge East and the tunnel; after that it was nearly all coasting home to Victoria. So it was at 3.48 p.m. we clanked our way across the points at the terminus, and came to a stand. I felt tired, my back and arms ached somewhat, but I had completed an interesting day's work. We were glad to see our relief and I reflected on the many times I had relieved an arriving main line train to do the dirty disposal work after; it was nice to be on the receiving end for once. Such was my introduction to Kent Coast express work.

The next two days were somewhat different, being back to disposal and preparation duties, except that one unusual bit of work was to take a light engine from Stewarts Lane to Nine Elms loco, which was due to visit Eastleigh Works. This was 34068 *Kenley* and was my first official visit to that depot which I was later to work from.

The following week saw me back on 13 duty again to complete my stint of third man working. Interestingly, I was to work on two different classes which gave a contrast to a King Arthur. In addition I was also to work with the redoubtable Charlie Stewart as the driver.

Charlie was a rough tough diamond. He was built in the traditional physique of the bouncer. Winter or summer, whatever the weather, his bull neck was open to the waist button of his shirt. To match this appearance, he also possessed the Honorary Doctorate of Profanities, for his conversation, although never boring, was terse and also liberal with what are euphemistically termed 'four letter words'. These were delivered in a loud and commanding voice, so there was no doubt who was in charge on his footplate.

On Monday 12th May, our engine on the 8.35 from Victoria was West Country 34104 *Bere Alston*. This in itself was fairly unusual for 34071 – 34110 were built with 5,500 gallon tenders compared with the 4,500 gallon tenders of the rest of the class and it was usual to use the smaller tender ones on the Ramsgate line (where water could be taken at a station en route) and the larger tender engines on the heavier non-stop boat train runs. No doubt at this time of the year, with boat train traffic reduced, some of the larger tender engines could be spared for the Ramsgate duty. So for this down run I sat and watched, except that for a couple of miles on the easier sections I was allowed to try my hand at firing, to get used to swinging the shovel right round at an angle of 90° to keep the back corners of the wide Pacific firebox filled – which was very different to firing the long box of the Arthurs. The other marked contrast to the latter on this first run I had on the light Pacifics was the speed. The Arthur plodded unremarkably on, riding fairly hard on the ground. The Pacific, dashed, rushed, flew and gave every impression of being somewhat impatient with its human controllers, seeming to want to go ever faster. Riding was of the Rolls Royce quality; however sharp the curve or rough the crossover, one seemed to float over. I have never before or since been on such a smooth-riding footplate; it was positively cushioned.

On arrival at Ramsgate we ran light to the loco and, as nearly all the graft had been performed by the fireman, I decided that I could at least do the lion's share of the disposal and preparation work to give him a rest. Although my intentions were good, in the long run on this occasion they gave more work and not less. I set about clearing the worst of it up, except for a large patch near the middle. It stubbornly adhered to the firebars. I hit it with the pricker and with the dart, to no avail. I started at it again with the pricker, hoping to get its tooth under the clinker and lift it off the bars. As it engaged I heaved and heaved, until – success! I felt it giving and I pulled even harder, then I peered into the box to see the results of my battle. Consternation! I had dragged a little of the clinker up but, in doing so, had also dislodged a firebar, which was what I had felt the pricker engage with and it now fell with a resounding clatter into the ashpan, leaving a large hole in the grate. I called the fireman up and confessed. He looked glum. Charlie meanwhile had been going round the outside of the engine, oiling the motion for the return run. He was summoned to the footplate to view the results of my labours. Having looked it over, he showered benedictions upon my head of a very dubious nature and we all proceeded to the Foreman to tell him what had happened.

There was nothing for it, we would have to leave 34104 with them, to drop the fire and repair the damage. He gave us a substitute engine to prepare for our return run. This was Schools class 30918 *Hurstpierpoint*. So we now had full preparation duties to carry out and poor Charlie, having nearly fully oiled the West Country, had to start all over again, with the addition of having to crawl into the middle motion to oil that up. Once again, I was on the receiving end of his congratulations!

An innovation which had taken place since I had been away was the adoption of the old Midland Railway and, subsequently, L.M.S.R. practice of shed number plates mounted on the smokebox and I noted that 30918 carried the Ramsgate plate of 74B. Before I had gone into the army, the Schools had also been green but since then they had been painted black, with the lining out reserved for secondary passenger engines. The result was most uninspiring compared with their former glory. Fortunately some years later they were at least to revert to B.R. green, which was a small mercy.

This time we had no Nottinghamshire coal to give us a start and the fire had to be built up from scratch with Kent coal. To do so meant building up the fire very gradually. Our return journey was certainly not as comfortable as with the Arthur, for the fire only gradually heated up and steam was not so ready to come by as on the previous run. By the time we had got to Faversham, we had another unpleasant surprise. The initial heap of coal at the front of the tender having been used up, we now found under it little but Kentish dust, which had to be fired very thinly to prevent it forming a crust-like top to the fire. It also caught the slightest breath of the wind or the slipstream of the engine, and whirled onto the footplate in minature dust-devils, coating everything and everybody liberally.

Going up Sole Street bank was a useful education, however, for with this dusty fuel it was very much a case of very little, very often, with Charlie opening and closing the firedoors as the fireman swung the shovel towards them, then closing them promptly as it was withdrawn. So, dusty, dirty and thankful the day was over, we ran into Victoria, only a couple of minutes late. The next day it was the same engine and crew; the following day, although it was *Hurstpierpoint* again, Charlie Stewart and his mate were rest day and the driver was Harry Wing. This time I was given my head and allowed to fire the whole way from Victoria to Ramsgate.

The contrast to the Arthur was marked. The Schools footplate was very compact; 5½″ less in width than the Arthurs, to enable the Schools to go through the restrictive Bo-Peep tunnel on the Hastings line. The distance from the tender to the firedoors was a little less, which made firing more comfortable, the distance on the Arthurs just verging on the long side. Although the overall impression was a smaller cab, I found it to be much more convenient than on the Arthurs, for everything seemed to be handy for various operations. This may not seem much but over the course of a couple of hours was a considerable amount of extra work. The injectors were the automatic restarting type and all that had to be done to operate them was to pull steadily and firmly on the steam handle against the spring pressure keeping the handle in the shut position. When in the fully opened position the injector would start, without having to adjust the overflow once the steam was on. To stop the injector it was just a case of pushing the handle back to its position without ceremony and water would be shut off as well. Pressure was 20 pounds higher than that the King Arthurs too, at 220 p.s.i., and although the reversing equipment was like the N15's the regulator – instead of being a copy of the L.S.W.R. type – was a large double-handle one across the footplate, easy to control from either side and very handy when operated from the driver's seat. The seats themselves were spring-loaded wooden ones, just big enough to sit on. When one stood, the spring shot them upwards flush with the inside of the cab out of the way – far better than the long fixed wooden box of the Arthurs, which was a minor nuisance when firing.

If the Arthurs steamed well, I found the steaming of the Schools was excellent and after a time there was a tendency to forget that the engine was only a 4-4-0. The only way the Schools were inferior to the Arthurs was their greater tendency to slip. The 4–6–0s were hardly known to do so but the Schools were very temperamental about losing their feet but again they were provided with steam chest pressure gauges, whereas the Arthurs (except those fitted with LeMaitre exhaust by Bulleid) were not. Careful handling of the regulator and observance of the steam chest gauge could obviate the worst of this tendency. The reason for this difference lay in the adhesion factor, (the ratio between the weight on the driving wheels and the tractive force of the engine); the heavier the engine in comparison with power, the less likely it was to slip and, of course, *vice versa* .The factor of the King Arthurs was 5.29 compared with the Schools 3.73. They were also lively on their springs which was particularly noticeable over points, a time when they were much more prone to movement up and down.

So ended my 'third man attachments' main line trips with three of the principal express classes of Southern Railway design. My general opinion was that the Arthurs were reliable without being in anyway outstanding; the light Pacifics were fast and furious, with a fairly healthy appetite for fuel; and that on the whole the Schools had a better turn of speed than their older cousins, and with moderate loads a comparable performance with the Pacifics. From the fireman's point of view on the Ramsgate turns, at least they were the best bet.

The next couple of days saw me in strange surroundings at unaccustomed 'office hour' times, taking the old Bucket South London line trains in the opposite direction to that I was used to, in attending the Firing School at

Bricklayers Arms loco, starting at 8 a.m. On the first day, it was a matter of lectures from Locomotive Inspectors, as well as films; and on the second more of the same, plus an address by the Divisional Motive Power Superintendent. On the whole, as far as I was concerned, I had to consider it a waste of time. . . .

But it was good to be back; the regimented days of army life were behind and an interesting future beckoned. It was a case of many happy returns to the old and the new.

CHAPTER EIGHT

Foreigners – man and machines

I was now available for any old duty that turned up, for coming back between roster adjustment, union agreements prohibited me from displacing anyone junior to me in a link until a general roster change took place. This occurred every three months. Until such a change, therefore, I was booked as spare without a rostered driver, being utilised by the duty clerk on any turn requiring a fireman. This period was to last just over a month and, although I expected to have to knuckle down to lots of shed preparation and disposal work, this did not happen I am glad to say. Actually I did only one day, this being the initial one on shed duties.

It was an interesting day, however, for my driver was A.J.Mills, who later was to be my rostered mate and, although preparing C class No.31580 and disposing Superheater 31749 was hardly anything out of the ordinary, our last job of the day was something else.

Harry Newman was a big man in every sense of the word, large of frame, with a perpetual twinkle in the eye, much more knowledgeable than many people suspected. Although he was one of the shed foremen he was universally liked, forever garbed in his black issue raincoat and looking like some oversized black crow as he swept into the lobby. He gave us our last job of the day, South Lambeth pilot, on the coal road, and then passed on to someone else. A somewhat unusual instruction, for usually you were given a piece of paper, with the number of the engine upon it, and instructions to either dispose or prepare it.

In the days of the old railway companies, many set up goods yards within the territories of other railways and the G.W.R. had a large yard only half a mile away up the line towards Victoria, South Lambeth yard. This was situated opposite Battersea Yard, on the other side of the line from Victoria and provided with a pilot engine throughout 24 hours of every day except Sunday. Much unproductive time was spent in transferring crews to and from Old Oak Common shed to man this pilot and after 1950, agreement had been reached that, although the engine would continue to be provided by Western Region, it would be crewed by Southern men. The engine would be changed over once per week by the new pilot working a train from Old Oak, the old engine working a goods train back. This engine, like all those with trains to and from this yard, was a 5700 class Pannier tank and for two hours every day it worked light engine back to Stewarts Lane to be readied for another day's work. Thus, as there was only one 5700 class likely to be on shed, Harry Newman did not need to identify the engine to us or tell us what to do; we had to dispose and prepare it and, after that, hand it over to the crew who would book on to do the next eight hours of shunting under the shadow of the famous Battersea Power station. So I boarded the first engine built by another railway company that I had the opportunity to work on. This was No.8770. I found her bunker-first to the hopper on the coal road. The first thing I had to do was move her back to the water crane. Knowing well that it is more important to be able to stop than to move, I searched round for the brake. The brake handle was an entirely unfamiliar object, completely different to the patented brakes that the Southern used. It consisted of an upright handle standing in the "off" position and could be moved to the left or right across the footplate. One side was marked for steam brake operation, the other for train pipe. I tried out both and heard the brakes apply when I put the handle to the steam brake position but, on moving it to the train pipe position, I also heard all sorts of weird noises. These were apparently connected with the G.W.R. Automatic Warning System and I decided at this juncture not to venture too far in my investigation of this contraption. Later, however, I did locate the very old fashioned small and large ejector handles which, unlike the Southern, were quite separate from the brake handle and experimented with them, managing to obtain that very rude raspberry sound, so typically Great Western. The cab seemed quite roomy for what from the outside seemed quite a small compact engine. Having mastered the brake, I blew the whistle (which was regulation practice before moving any engine, to warn anyone in the vicinity) and opened the regulator after pulling back the heavy stick lever to the reverse position. The engine moved back with a typical throaty exhaust, being much quieter in travel than the South Eastern or Brighton tanks I was used to. Experimentally trying the steam brake I found it to be very sharp and responsive and so I brought her to a stand at the water crane. Putting in the hose, I retraced my steps to the ground, turned on the water at a slow rate and then set about disposing the engine. I found that, like the Southern, there was nothing modern or labour saving in this direction; it was shovel out smokebox ash, shovel out clinker, rake out the ashpan, etc. At length, Driver Mills having joined me, we trundled back under the coal stage, filled the bunker, made the fire up and reloaded more coal into the bunker and then ran round through the Green Yard back to the outlet side of the loco. When we got relieved and left her I was slightly bemused; obviously a good traditional design of engine but was it really necessary to have everything on the footplate looking as Victorian as though Gooch had just designed it last week? I was to come into contact with Panniers in greater earnest later.

The rest of that week and the next were like old times, for my next three days work to complete the week were spent back on the old E2 tanks again, although this time on the Stewarts Lane Goods Yard pilot. Now the old T class tanks had been scrapped, the E2s had taken over their duties in addition to all their former ones. 32102 was the engine on the turn for the three days and was carrying the inscription BRITISH RAILWAYS in full in Southern Railway style on the tanks. The following week took me into familiar ground on night duties, for I booked on at 11.15 on Sunday night to work a W 2-6-4T on two trips to Norwood, the 12.45 and 4.15 a.m. trips, returning with the 2.45 and 6.20 from Norwood. On preparing the engine, it turned out to be a rush job, for after about 20 minutes into the preparation of 31912, Phil Warner, my driver for the night, found one of the sand pipes missing, so we were told to take 31915 instead. On getting on the footplate, I found that the fire had only been lit some three or four hours before and boiler pressure stood at 10 pounds per square inch; however, she was on the boil for opening the blower, lifting the smoke coming back from the firehole into the cab, and by the time we were due to depart from the loco at fifteen minutes after midnight about 100 pounds was showing on the gauge. As we had only to trundle to Battersea Yard and had about twenty minutes' wait there, it gave time to get a full head of steam. Such close calls made life a bit hectic at times.

The following six nights were all on the Victoria pilot, very much back to the time when I started firing, again with an H class tank. Most nights the engine varied but 31005 was on the turn for two nights. She was an interesting engine, the lowest numbered tank engine of S.E.C.R. origin taken over by the Southern, being No.5 of that railway. Although painted black, she had been one of the earliest examples of lining out in mixed traffic livery on British Railways, which suited her very well, although she was far from being a mixed traffic engine. This treatment proved to be a thorough job for she did not require repainting for several years and so remained distinct from her black unlined sisters.

Throughout the inner suburban area of Southern Region, electric traction reigned supreme on all passenger services, except for one sole exception. This was a steam-worked service from Clapham Junction to Kensington (Olympia), which ran during the rush hours only, non-stop between those two stations. It was provided principally for the use of a large S.P.O. establishment at Kensington and this unique service had also some unique rolling stock. The South Eastern & Chatham Railway in 1905 introduced eight railcars. They saw active service for up to 15 years, when they were laid aside and the Southern Railway in due course scrapped their engines and converted the coaching part of four of them into a pair of two-coach articulated sets. After being used on various branch lines, both sets of coaches were brought together (Sets 513 and 514) and kept at Clapham Junction to form the Kensington train. They were saloon-type, with large windows, rode very well and were at this time painted in the all-over red of secondary passenger stock, with the set numbers prominently painted on the ends in gold. Great pride was taken in the appearance of these vehicles, which were kept spotless inside and out by the Clapham Junction staff. Prior to my Army service, I had worked this train now and again, when the motive power was usually one of the "Bobtail" R1 tanks or perhaps an H class. My reintroduction to the working, however, proved also to be an introduction to another 'Foreign' class that Stewarts Lane had inherited, this time in the shape of the L.M.S. Ivatt-designed 2P 2-6-2 tanks.

These had been introduced by that company in 1946, with the intention of making them a standard class to replace the collection of ageing pre-Grouping designs still working most of the many branch line services. Progress had been slow in building them, however, only ten having been completed by Nationalisation. British Railways decided at an early stage to go ahead with quantity production of them until a suitable B.R. Standard design was ready, and a further 120 were built between 1949-52. Most went to the former L.M.S. areas but 40 (numbered 41290 to 41329) came new to the Southern. Of these the first nine were different from the rest; in place of the usual parallel chimney, they were fitted with a small tapered chimney, slightly reminiscent of a Drummond one. Stewarts Lane was provided with eight of these nine, the last one (41298) going to Bricklayers Arms.

So it was that on the morning of Tuesday 3rd June 1952, at about 6.30 a.m., I clambered onto the footplate of 41290, as my introduction to working, L.M.S. style. The L.M.S. had in fact more than any other railway taken standardisation of design to almost an extreme, which it was claimed was both cost and performance effective, so I was very interested in what I was going to find out personally about this philosophy.

I must say I was impressed from the start. Weighing only 9 tons more than the H class, the cab was neat, large for so small an engine, and provided with much more cover from the elements than we were used to. Sliding glass windows were fitted which could be shut to exclude high winds and rain, an unimagined luxury so far as our own engines were concerned. In stormy conditions in exposed places, the only solution was to stand up close to the firebox using the side cab sheeting as some protection from the elements. Even then, sudden gusts laden with rain would enter the cab and so a head-down stance was also adopted to use the peak of the cap to shield the face! Seating too was much improved. The tip-up wooden seat was comfortable and situated right against the cab side sheets, so that sitting normally it was possible to look out in the direction of travel without leaning to one side. On our smaller tanks, to increase water capacity the tanks were brought right inside the cab, which consequently involved some contortions sideways at times to get a clear view outside.

Reversal was by screw, as with the 4P tanks, whilst small and large ejector handles were fitted to release the train brakes. This was not as good as the Southern designs, for Crewe used an ancient, cheap, nasty and slow type of ejector, which took something like half a minute or more to release train brakes compared to the much more effective Davies & Metcalfe design commonly used by us. Braking of the engine was steam, used in combination with the vacuum ejector. From the fireman's point of view, controls were handy; water controls for the injectors were placed under the seat area and the steam handles were well placed, with 200 pounds pressure of superheated steam as a maximum, compared with our more normal of 160 saturated. Again, however, there was one strange drawback. On Southern engines the train steam heating valve was supplied with a normal handle, so that it could be turned on immediately and up to 60 p.s.i. could be pushed into the train heating before the safety valve mounted in the cab blew off; on the 2Ps, however, no handle was fitted, only a square on the end of the valve, which required use of a spanner before it could be turned and pressure was limited to 40 p.s.i. maximum. Moreover, that pressure came down rapidly with any drop of boiler pressure. The ashpan handles were positive sliding controls on a quadrant, much better than older S.E.C.R. controls which consisted of a bar pulled up or down. The only other control I did not like was in fact the blower. On most Southern designs this was placed very nearly in front of either the driver or the fireman, so that in the event of a blowback from the firebox it could be readily operated. On L.M.S. engines it was placed just above the firehole door and I could envisage difficulty in getting to it if flames and smoke were blowing back, although in fact it was something I did not experience on them and additionally substantial and easily worked firedoors were provided.

After doing the usual checks, I opened the damper and was surprised by two things – how dull and lifeless the fire looked when the damper was closed, indicating very airtight dampers and how quickly the fire came to life once opened. This looked a good omen, for it indicated good draughting.

My driver on this week's work was a cheerful fellow called Monty. Just after seven we ran light engine to a siding on the old Brighton side of Clapham Junction and coupled onto our ex-railcar stock. We had about half an hour's stand before propelling them back into the Central Section platforms. I had found that steaming appeared to be good, although light engine working is no gauge, for so little steam is used. On the strength of what I had seen I had kept the dampers closed in the siding and found confirmation of my earlier observations for steam rose by only about five pounds per square inch in half an hour. When we started back into the station, the dampers were still closed and from the initial exhaust of steam, the only way air could be drawn through the firebox was via the doors. Sure enough, the air passing through them rattled them prodigiously, as many cubic feet of air passed through the small vents built into the doors, and ceased to do so as soon as I opened the damper. Starting away from the Junction down the slope curving under the Western Section main line and onto the West London Extension Railway, pressure dropped from 200 pounds to 180 but then the fire heated up and on this three mile run I could see that I was not going to have to do any firing, for soon pressure was heading rapidly upwards again, despite the engine being worked quite hard, with a nice crisp yet throaty exhaust. As we approached the Thames, I prevented the valves lifting by putting on the injector and in eight minutes, after passing under the Earls Court exhibition building, we clattered into Kensington. Running round our train, after being uncoupled and recoupled by the Western Region shunter, we were off back to the Junction nine minutes later.

Back we came to Clapham Junction and this time the turnround was only eight minutes. All the actual firing on this turn could be done at the terminal points, in fact all the action took place there, for after running-round it was my job also to change the headboards from back to front and vice versa. Away again and, after completing our second trip, we ran round again and off in eight minutes. It all seemed a whirl once started and was really to and fro, run round, off again, giving a slight impression of giddiness. This time, after arriving at Clapham Junction, we propelled the stock back into the siding and the rest of the day was recovery time, for we now trundled over to the Windsor sidings, the other side of the station to work for the rest of the shift as station pilot.

The rest of the week was the same turn with the same engine. They were beauties, these new engines. They had various nick names throughout the country; on the Southern they acquired the name "Teddy Bears". I think it says it all – warm and cuddly, with no vices.

The following Sunday was a good example of the somewhat traumatic existence a fireman could have due to absenteeism and I had a somewhat bruising experience in another way.

I had booked on at 8.00 a.m. to prepare a Teddy Bear and then work a couple of empty stock trains from Stewarts Lane sidings to Victoria, the second of these being the 10.20 empties for the Golden Arrow.

As soon as I booked on, however, the Running Foreman was waiting for me. "I want you to prepare 35028 straight away," he said and told me he had run short of firemen, with no one to prepare the Merchant Navy for a boat train. Preparing a Merchant was one of the hardest tasks going, so I set to with a will and an hour later had completed the task. Meanwhile, a passed cleaner had prepared my own engine, 41293, so I got off 35028 as soon as the boat train fireman booked on and onto my own engine to run light to the carriage sidings. To do this an outlet shunt signal was cleared and the engine worked out of the loco, over a pair of points and, after the points had been changed, move forward again and into the sidings. Sometimes more than one light engine at a time had to do this move, so in this situation it was permissive block working. This meant that the shunt signal, when clear, indicated that permission had been given to proceed but that another engine might be in the section, so movement should be at a slow speed and a sharp lookout kept for any other engine. We backed out over the points and I turned with brush in hand to sweep some coal dust from the floor. I had just started brushing when I had the sensation of suddenly becoming detached from the floor and the firebox hurtling towards me from about four feet distant, whilst at the same time coal dust descended in clouds from the roof and coal hole, and jerked up from the floorboards. All this being accompanied by a loud bang. As I hit the firebox, I felt a sharp pain in the arm above the left elbow and fell to a heap on the floor.

Harry Martin, my driver, had been flung forward over the reverser but had something to hang onto, so was little the worse for wear. I staggered to my feet still not knowing what had happened but very fully aware of an intense pain in my left arm. Collapsing onto my seat, I stared forward through the front spectacle plate to observe a King Arthur standing a few feet ahead of our engine, tender foremost. They had followed us out past the shunt signal but had certainly not kept a good look out, and had hit us at about 10 m.p.h. Fortunately our brakes were off and some of the shock had been absorbed by propelling us several yards backwards. Tom Stuckley was the driver and as he clambered up to us I had removed my overall top to reveal a blue-black and yellow bruise, giving the clear outline of the blower handle on my anatomy. "You all right, matey?" he asked. Tom was never really one to say he was in the wrong, although his visit to us was a silent acknowledgement that this was so. I did feel shaken and a bit sick but having gingerly prodded the wound, I thought nothing was broken. We decided we ought not to obstruct the line further, so *Sir Bors de Ganis* rode forth from the fray, having certainly for the moment vanquished me. We followed at a respectable distance, and though my arm was still painful I decided I could carry on, so shortly after we departed with our twelve Pullmans and the train engine in the rear up the hill to Grosvenor Bridge and Victoria. Little did I know, however, that my tribulations were not entirely over for the day. We ran light back to Stewarts Lane after banking out the Arrow and as we went in, my good friend the Running Inspector again accosted me, this time in quite apologetic mood, for he was aware that I had already done half a shift, helped him out once and received a clout for good behaviour. "I've got no one for the Newhaven Boat", he said, indicating Schools No.30922 *Marlborough,* which had been prepared by a passed cleaner with no main line experience, so once more I exchanged footplates, got onto the Schools and the outlet signal cleared for Victoria. Just as we were about to move, the foreman's phone rang. We had started to move when he ran out of the office and gave me a hand signal to stop. "Hang on," he said. "I've just had someone book on who can take it." Saved by the bell! So back again to 41293 and to the last part of the duty. The Stewarts Lane pilot shunted our train of milk tanks onto us, which was for Clapham Junction and Kensington. We propelled this back onto the main and then reversed up the slope past Hampton's Depository to Longhedge Junction. The home signal on the gantry was on, so we stood there about five minutes awaiting the signal. As it cleared and Harry Martin opened the regulator, he called out to me that someone was on the track ahead near the bridge over Queenstown Road. I poked my head out just in time to get into the photograph taken nearly 30 years ago on page 69.

Talking of footplate mishaps, the next day I worked with Dave Humphries, who experienced what must rank as one of the most terrible and ill-fated footplate disasters of this century. Dave at that time was a fresh-faced pleasant man, I suppose in his late thirties but the effect of his experience always seemed to be somehow with him and no one ever discussed it with him.

On 16th August 1944 Dave Humphries was the fireman of a Ramsgate express, the engine being a King Arthur. At that time hundreds of flying bombs were being launched across the Channel against London and the south-east of England. Many were shot down by fighters. Another way of bringing them down, particularly over remote areas, was for fighters to fly alongside them and tip the wings of the bomb with the aircraft wings; this caused the bombs to crash and explode in areas of sparse population. Such was the case in the Rainham area of Kent, when on the Gillingham side of the station a pilot tipped one bomb and it plunged to earth. Unfortunately it crashed onto a bridge on the main line and blew it out. The pilot then saw to his horror an express approaching. Only at the last moment did the crew realise the position. An emergency application of the brake was made but the engine and first two coaches jumped the gap, becoming derailed on the far side, the remaining coaches falling down into the void or coming to a stand in the wreckage. Dave was severely injured and took months to recover. In all eight people were killed and sixteen seriously hurt with many more suffering lesser injuries. A sequel to it was that when rescue efforts had been completed, one person was not accounted for, the driver. He was found two days later by one of his colleagues in a dirty and dishevelled condition wandering aimlessly about Clapham Junction station and when he eventually recovered he was unable to recall how he came to be there. . . .

On 16th June I returned to the main line, travelling down passenger on a train behind L class 31764, driven by Tom Stuckey. I made my way to Ramsgate loco with Jack May and with 30792 *Sir Hervis de Revel* ran light to Margate sidings, where we picked up our train, a ten coach special, working away at 7.55 in the evening to Victoria. Now I had the full responsibility and, although I now had plenty of experience, there were still butterflies in the stomach as we started away. But she went like a good 'un, an old dependable slogging Arthur and we ran into Victoria on time.

Another foreigner came my way shortly afterwards on a Sunday. It was, in fact, exactly two weeks after my pitch-in on 41293 and on this occasion I was involved in a somewhat similar incident, except that this time I was the culprit. It was one of those detestable turns; preparing main line engines, running them to Victoria, getting relieved, bringing another one back, disposing and so on. All dirty, hard work, with very little of interest, except the first part of No.3 duty, which was just a little part of the most illustrious duty at Stewarts Lane, for this was the turn which worked the Golden Arrow. My responsibilities were to prepare the engine for duty, then run round to the carriage sidings, hook onto the back of the train, bank and run to

In June 1961 the author recalls former days, on the footplate of H15 class 30524.

The footplate of a King Arthur (No. 30788 **Sir Urre of the Mount***) viewed from the firemans side.*

Victoria. There we would be relieved by the top link crew, who were to work the train to Dover. On this day the engine for the turn was the normal one, 70004 *William Shakespeare.* She was always in spotless condition and invariably cleaned every day under the watchful eye of Bob Strange, the cleaner chargeman, every day that is except sometimes on Sundays, when cleaners were not always available.

In fact this was part of my undoing on this particular Sunday, for possibly in anticipation that the cleaners would not need her out in the open, 70004 had been shedded overnight in the recesses of the shed at the top of 2 road. Our shed was one of the gloomiest inside. The roof was fairly lofty and dirty and the inadequate lamps were few and far between, as well as soot-begrimed. With Bulleid Pacifics, if some work had to be done in the shed, it was of no great consequence, for the electric generator could be turned on and good lighting was immediately available on the footplate. All other engines, including the Standard classes, did not have this useful facility and in daylight it was preferable immediately to move them from the dark and smoky depths to the roads outside the shed for preparation.

Wally Upsher was my driver and as I had arrived for work a little early, he had not booked on when I boarded the Britannia. There was no engine on the road in the shed but standing outside in the last stages of preparation was a U1 class; there was plenty of room for me to move the Britannia out clear into the open air. In fact, it was not the first time I had been on the footplate of this particular engine, although the last occasion was in very different circumstances. She had been one of the British Railways exhibits in the Pavilion of Engineering on the South Bank during the Festival of Britain before she entered service. I had looked over her sister engine, 70014, since I had returned but this was my first work in earnest on the class. A lot of thought had gone into the layout of the cab, with a very neat layout and everything to hand. The firebox front on the footplate was completely lagged and covered in, unlike many engines where this was only partly done; although this did make the footplate look much neater, it had a drawback from the crew point of view, for very little heat came onto the footplate and it was found in practice that a somewhat unpleasant draught came from under the footplate doors. In the winter on the road these Pacifics could thus be rather cool to work on — particularly so compared to the heat generated on the footplate of the Bulleid engines.

I decided to move the 4-6-2 out and in the gloom found the ejector handle which, like L.M.S. practice, was separated from the brake handle. I knocked it up and saw the train pipe pressure rise immediately to the required 21″. The brake handle was a smart chromium-plated affair sitting on a little desk-like top, conveniently situated in front of the driver at hip level. To the right of it was what I always thought of myself as the bacon slicer. The reverser was of the screw type but, instead of the usual wheel mounted in front of the driver, it was a much more sensible affair, mounted just like a bacon slicer handle and turned in the same manner — wound away from you for forward movement and towards you for reverse. I wound it towards me and, having taken the handbrake off previously, reached out in the gloom for the whistle handle in front of me. The tone of the Britannia whistle is well known and I must admit it was a very melodious instrument. Loco men are as partial to good music as the next man, so it did get somewhat overworked. I felt like the cat's whiskers as I gave a long blow on the whistle to warn all nearby that the engine was about to move, then felt in front of me for the regulator, clenched my hand round the handle and pulled back towards me. Steam hissed and the forward view disappeared as we moved back with the cylinder cocks open; after a couple of seconds came the measured deep exhaust from the chimney which could be felt as well as heard. What a grand life in charge of such a monster as this, moving under my command; the feeling of power, personal power was ego-filling! I looked back along the tender in the direction we were going and shut the regulator, we slowed just slightly and I saw there was some way to go yet to the outside of the shed. I could give her a bit more steam. I opened the regulator again. I had let things go to my head a little, however, and opened it a bit on the heavy side; still no matter, a bit of brake would check her down. I could now see I was about to emerge into the open and was getting quite a bit closer to the U-boat outside. Confidently I moved the brake handle towards the application position and the air started to hiss into the holes and so into the train pipe. Strange! The engine didn't seem to be slowing. Perhaps those brakes needed a fairly heavy application. I applied more brake. Nothing was happening. Panic! Emergency application. Still nothing happened. Real panic! I gave a swift glance back and saw the distance to the 2-6-0 outside was rapidly diminishing. I decided in a flash to move the reverser to the forward position and open the regulator to stop the rearward movement by brute force. In my excitement, however, I fumbled the catch on the reverser which was locking it in the rearward position, something that quite often happened in normal times. There was little time left to do much else, so I grasped the whistle handle and pumped it furiously. Short sharp blasts rent the air and I saw a head poke out from the cab of the 2-6-0 with which collision was imminent. Bang! I had instinctively held onto the window framing as we hit, the clang of the buffers crashing, being accompanied by a shuddering of the side plates of the tender as the shock was transmitted. The engine ran right into the tender and then back forwards about a foot, coming to a stand as the rebound momentum became spent. I can still recall this incident with the utmost clarity, etched in the memory due to the drama of the experience. For about a second afterwards everything was quiet and nothing moved, including myself. What had happened to the crew on the other engine? The U1 was a three-cylinder engine - had that most unspeakable thing happened that sometimes killed footplatemen, the engine moving whilst the inside motion was being oiled? Cases had occurred with men mangled to death by the inside motion moving. Were we and the other engine still on the rails? This was the Golden Arrow engine; had it suffered damage? Was I for the high jump? Why had the Britannia stopped?

I shakily jumped down from the footplate and made my way to the other engine. Two men were on the footplate. Both looked down on me with utter scorn on their faces. Thankful they were there at all, I stumbled words of apology and was to some extent reassured by the torrent of unprintable language I received in reply. At least my pumping had some success, for the driver had looked out, seen the collision was imminent, shouted to his mate to hang on and their brakes had been off waiting to move away. The driver had attempted to open the regulator to get away from the collision but contact had been made before he could do so. With trembling knees I now went to the gap between the two engines and first surveyed the gleaming, silvery buffers of the Brittannia; they had hit fair and square and were undamaged. Then a look at the other engine. It too was okay. I concluded the devil had looked after his own; no damage, no injury. I returned to the footplate and immediately in the full light of day saw the explanation staring fully at me. A steam brake lever stood on the boiler back at eye level. All the ejector did was empty a train pipe connected to nothing. It was vacuum for the train and separate steam brake for the engine. . . .

About a week earlier I was disappointed to see that on the new roster I had been placed in No.7 link from 23rd June, with Fred Davis as my driver. I was none too happy, for I had hoped to be a little higher up; this was the last link consisting of round-the-houses and such like turns. The most interesting probably was a goods working from Norwood Junction to Wimbledon on the Western Section via Waddon Marsh, which involved staff working on the single line section between Mitcham Junction and Merton Park. This was a very rural branch in the heart of suburbia. It ended in the evening shunting at the long-disused passenger station at Merton Abbey, from which passenger facilities had been with-drawn in 1926 but there was still a considerable amount of coal traffic and a fair bit of traffic from sidings to Lines Brothers factory, the producers of Triang toys. The engine was always a C class on this turn, the heaviest class allowed on the branch, and the day's work terminated working a train back to Herne Hill via Wimbledon and Tooting.

A few weeks after I joined No.7 link, I was booked for a turn for one week starting at the unearthly hour of 3.20 a.m. It entailed empty stock working and pilot duties. All the week we had a 2P tank, except for one odd day when we had H class 31321, and I think that the following snippet of our working that day will illustrate what an outstandingly BIG little engine they were. I have always been a fervent admirer of them.

Platform 2 at Victoria is capable of holding twelve coaches with a locomotive at each end. Picture then this platform occupied almost to the starting signal, with no engine at the stops end, the train consisting of no less than 25 vehicles of 4,6, and 8-wheel types which had accumulated from the night parcels and mail trains. This, in fact, had been a very much busier night than usual and on other nights the loads had been very much less. To work this cavalcade, weighing over 350 tons, up the twisting bank to Grosvenor Bridge, required an engine of some power and we had only our 0-4-4 tank 31321 to work this train to Stewarts Lane carriage sidings. The crew of the station pilot, an E2 tank standing on No.1 platform, had no doubts about the impossibility of such a task and bet us we would stall on the bank - in fact, the fireman started to shovel coal into the firebox to get up steam ready for that event.

This was the challenge we needed; we didn't fancy our chances either, but we were determined to try.

I got a full head of steam, full boiler and, as the starting signal cleared, put the blower full on, to get the fire as hot as possible even when standing. Right away! Full regulator was used, with the sand on to keep our feet. She gave a half slip with all this power and load but gradually, with an enormously loud exhaust, measured but slowly increasing in frequency, we pulled away. A little cut-off was possible, which helped the front end to get rid of steam and not be slowed by back pressure but, as soon as we hit the adverse grade, it had to be full gear again. Only doing about 20 m.p.h., we barked up the slope, slower and slower, down to 10 m.p.h. as we levelled with the roof of the Eastern Carriage sheds. The bridge looked to be an awful long way away. The wheels were literally grinding on the rails at our faltering speed but at last we reached the bridge, down to about 5 m.p.h. and still perceptibly slowing. The exhaust was back to measured blasts, with a clear second of silence between them. I had not dared put on the injector because every pound of steam counted, although water consumption with such heavy working had taken its toll of the level in the boiler and showed to be well below half a glass. It was literally a puff at a time and then gradually, gradually, we began gaining momentum. It was then a case of putting on both injectors for the coming steep downgrade past Battersea Park; we didn't want to have got so far and then drop a fusible plug on the far side. By the time we approached the far end of the bridge, we knew we had won our bet. Yes, the H class were great little engines – the Bluebell Railway must be proud of theirs.

Another engine was doing less well at Victoria at this time. The L.M.S.R. had produced, just before the end of their existence, a Bo-Bo diesel-electric numbered 10800 and it was given a trial on the Tunbridge Wells trains. It once passed us when we worked a Norwood Goods with a W class 2-6-4T, near Thornton Heath on a down train, struggling against the odds hauling five coaches. We thought it great fun seeing such a pathetic performance; we were sure these new-fangled diesels would never take on!

At this time there were lots of little things of interest too numerous to mention but one, for instance, was the last time I fired a Southern Railway numbered engine. This was our P class tank 1558; with Fred Davis, I fired her on the Milk Pilot on 23rd August 1952, when she was still in full Southern Railway livery. She was, in fact, the last engine to remain so, eventually being repainted and renumbered in B.R. style on 25th July the following year.

CHAPTER NINE

"Wiggo" and Driving

Another roster. This time, however, things were different; I didn't move up a link but remained in No.7. Fred Davis moved up and this resulted in a new driver coming into the place he had vacated. My new mate was J. Wiggs. To this day I don't know what the J. stood for, because he was known to all and sundry as Wiggo. Frankly, to me the change was welcome. Personalities count in all walks of life and particularly where team work is concerned – and if anything was team work, footplate work certainly was. Fred Davis was in his mid fifties and, although we could say we got on alright, I think we would have agreed that there was no great meeting of minds. Fred was more interested in arriving at the end of the working day than anything else. His interest in the job was minimal and, on one occasion when he had allowed me to drive a 2P tank, he accused me of running light engine without having a power brake available. This was due to his ignorance of the braking system of the engine we were working. I replied by immediately applying the power brake, which very nearly sent him sprawling and he was lost for words due to the surprise.

Wiggo, however, was very different. First of all, there was not the age difference that had existed between Fred and me, for Wiggo was in his late twenties. He was small of stature, very quick and wiry, both physically and mentally. We promised to be well suited as a team, which in the fullness of time proved to be the case. You might be curious, however, as to how such a junior man in service had been appointed as a driver halfway up the links in the shed. The answer was that he was a dual link man. I think this method of working was unique to the Southern. With its vast amount of suburban and main line electrification there were, of course, depots exclusively for electric motormen. An instance was Streatham Common, which came under the responsibility of the Shedmaster at Stewarts Lane and they, like the steam sheds, had a few spare men to cover sickness and absenteeism etc. There was also a requirement to cover annual leave, long term sickness and the like and a further pool of men was required for this purpose. This was provided by the dual link. Men in this were recruited from qualified steam drivers who were then trained to drive electrics. Afterwards they were returned to their steam shed, covering electric jobs as required. It had been found, however, that men did not readily come forward for this dual link, most passed firemen opting to remain at steam sheds and take promotion as steam drivers. In order, therefore, to encourage entry into the dual link, there was a preferential system which promoted men faster in the steam links than those that opted for steam work only. There was only one snag to this; eventually, as permanent vacancies occurred at electric depots, the dual link men would fill them as motormen, severing their connection with steam for ever. It is interesting to speculate why the dual link was unpopular and men had to be encouraged to become motormen. I think the answer was twofold. Men who had always had a mate to talk to on the footplate found the motorman's job rather solitary. In addition, despite the dirt and dust of the footplate, steam work was preferred to electric because it had a greater prestige. So far as I was concerned, therefore, it would mean that when my mate was required for electric duties, I would have another driver teamed up with me.

The first day of the new roster was Sunday 14th September, 1952, the last Sunday of the year for seaside excursion traffic. We would be able to judge each other's capabilities on this first day, as we had just such a train to work. This judgement was never spoken of but always took place – each seeing what kind of mate he had been lumbered or blessed with as the case might be.

We booked on at 9.35 a.m., our engine having been prepared for us. But before finding out what it was there was something else to interest me. There were strangers on the shed, in the form of 75019, a standard class 4MT 2-6-0 from Southport shed on L.M. Region; Southern Main line diesel 10202; and diesel shunter 12120, newly delivered from Derby. They had arrived to go on display in an exhibition which was opened a few days later in Battersea Yard, joined there by Western Region Britannia 70025, appropriately named *Western Star*. After a quick look at them, we proceeded to our engine, 31743, a Superheater.

We departed light engine from the shed at 9.50 and ran to Bellingham on the Catford loop, where we backed onto the coaches in the siding. During the summer in steam days, sets of coaches were kept in various sidings or goods yards for excursion or special trains. This was a good arrangement for it freed the London terminal stations to accommodate more important extras and dispensed with the requirement for an extra locomotive to work the empty stock. It also provided a train for passengers proceeding from suburban stations to the sea, for instance, our empties we worked about four miles distant to Bromley South, where we entrained passengers for the Kent Coast resorts. Most of the coaching stock, of course, was not in the prime of youth; in this case it was a set of eight "Ironclads", which had originally been built for S.E.C.R. Continental traffic just before the Grouping. Sometimes it was a train of S.E.C.R. non-corridor "Birdcage" stock more suited to branch line working than the lengthy journeys involved in these circumstances.

We left Bromley South in good style, rousing the echoes climbing up to Bickley, for starting away on the adverse gradient required heavy working of the Superheater. These rebuilds could shout even louder than an Arthur. The trip was no trouble, the climb up to Swanley, the up and down of the undulations through Farningham Road and Meopham and then the headlong descent down to the Medway towns, touching 80 on the way. The train was for Ramsgate but we got relieved on arrival at Faversham at 12.17.

In contrast to most turns of this type this was a holiday, for we now had over two hours to have some refreshments and then relax a little before relieving an up train at 2.50. We found this time we had an Arthur, Stewarts Lane No.30769, *Sir Balan*. At 2.52 we promptly departed to Victoria. This train had started from Deal, called at all stations to Chatham, then ran fast to Bromley South and Victoria. We arrived there at 4.42. Again the trip gave us no anxiety, for 30769 was like all the Lane Arthurs – dependable. In any case, the fairly frequent stops would have enabled me to bring her round to a full head of steam should things not have gone so well. So we completed our first trip. The final judgement would depend upon how we handled things when they were not going well.

Doubtless all steam enthusiasts mourn the passing of steam but there can be no doubt the advantages to passengers in general at the introduction of electric trains. If one takes into account the journey just described, we were allowed 110 minutes for the 52 miles to Victoria, an average speed of 28 m.p.h. An electric train covering the same route and stopping at the same 10 stations is now allowed 72 minutes, an average speed of 43 m.p.h. and at no doubt a reduced operating cost when compared to steam.

The next couple of weeks were nothing special; mostly short distance shunting, goods turns or running main line engines to and from Victoria, disposing and preparing them. On the Tuesday of the following week, I ran Schools 30917 *Ardingly* back from Victoria to dispose, then prepare and run back again and my notes record that when I went to empty the smokebox, I found a dead sparrow lying on the buffer beam. Now and again we did find birds had not been quick enough and been hit by engines; by repute, partridges were particularly prone to this, although I had never had the good fortune to find one. Dead wildlife seemed so out of place on the hot front of an engine, I must admit I always felt a twinge of remorse when I found them, hence I suppose my diary note. The most puzzling episode in this respect was finding a large fully-grown badger gently smouldering on the positive conductor rail at Herne Hill sidings. It was far from the country and we were completely non-plussed as to how it came to be there.

Doing the sort of turns just described could mean working on a large number of engines of varying classes in a short space of time, much of it very heavy and unpleasant work on preparation and disposal duties. In those first two weeks, for instance, we worked on no less than 20 engines of the following classes: Battle of Britain, Schools, King Arthur, U1 D1 E1 and 2P.

On the second Sunday following our Faversham trip, we booked on at 10.05 p.m. for the night milk run. At this date, milk was almost exclusively moved long distances throughout the country by train, in milk tank-wagons, whereas now of course this is largely a thing of the past and is very largely a road operation. Stewarts Lane had what could be termed the local delivery end of this operation.

A milk train from north Devon and Dorset arrived nightly at Clapham Junction a little after midnight. It was there divided into a number of portions. One went to a rail-served depot at Mottingham; another to Vauxhall, where pipes mounted on the platform were provided to pump the milk from the station into the nearby bottling depot; and a third portion was worked to Stewarts Lane, where the milk pilot mentioned in previous chapters shunted it round to the C.W.S. plant.

In addition to this supply, a Western Region train worked into Wood Lane milk depot, which had a connection on to the West London Extension railway a little north of Olympia, some of these tanks being worked on to Stewarts Lane. At other times, further supplies were also picked up at Olympia as well.

On this particular night we prepared our engine (2P 41296) and then ran from the loco into Stewarts Lane goods yard. We worked the 11.10 to Victoria, which comprised empty vans for the night newspaper mail and parcel traffic for Kent. At 11.40 it was light back to Stewarts Lane again to work vans to Clapham Junction, departing ten minutes after midnight. After stowing the vans in the Windsor sidings, we picked up our first milk train of the night which the pilot, an M7 tank, had detached from the main train for us. These we worked to Stewarts Lane and, leaving them in the charge of the milk pilot, we again gathered more vans of J. Lyons and at 2.10 a.m. left with these for Olympia. This firm at this time had a considerable cake traffic from there to all parts of the country. After leaving them in the care of the G.W.R. 5700 class pilot, we backed onto some milk tanks again and at this juncture Wiggo asked me if I would like to do the driving. I accepted with alacrity.

After we had been hooked up, the signal being clear for our departure, I opened the regulator and away we went. The "Teddy Bears", as well as being pleasant engines to fire, were equally good to drive. Seated, the regulator was at one's right hand, at about hip high when closed – very conveniently placed to grasp and pull upwards to open. The reverser was immediately in front of the seat, so that it was very easy to release the lock with one hand and turn to the required position with the other, then relock. The cut-off scale was engraved in large characters on the top, so that its position could be taken in at a glance.

We expected usually a nonstop run at this time of night. We passed the District Line station at West Brompton, then the darkened and deserted Chelsea football ground, the bright coke ovens of the gas works on the north bank of the Thames, and rumbled over the river bridge. I was enjoying my driving stint, looking out for the semaphore signals, which on this stretch of the railway were all G.W.R. lower quadrant (and mostly still are to this day), although at this time of night it was only the spectacles that were observable from a distance. After passing onto the south bank, we approached Latchmore Junction box. Here the line divided, the right hand forking away to Clapham Junction and the Western and Central sections, the left hand to the Eastern section. To my surprise all signals were at danger. I closed the regulator, wound the reverser forward and gently moved the brake handle across the faceplate until a faint hiss of air entering the brake pipe told me the brakes were gradually applying. As we approached the home signal, it remained resolutely at danger, so a slightly heavier application of brake was required, bringing us to a stand. The signal then cleared and, as I opened the regulator, I observed that the signalman in the box some two hundred yards ahead of us was moving to the top of the outside stairs with his handlamp at the ready. As we neared, he shone a red handsignal towards us, so I shut off and gave a brake application to bring us to a stand to within a few feet of him. "Know you've got no headlamps?" he queried. Was our collective face red! As the fireman, it had been my job to transfer the lamps from the bunker to the front but as my mate had handed over to me it could also be said to have been his job, as we had swapped roles. However, as it was not usually done by him, again the onus fell back on me. So I departed bunkerwards and scrambled about in the dark transferring them to their rightful position on the front of the engine, then back to the footplate. I suitably apologised to the signalman, then opened the regulator to resume our progress.

Arriving at Stewarts Lane Goods yard without further incident at 3.25 a.m., we there became the goods yard pilot with a little desultory shunting called for until we were relieved at 5.25 a.m. – and so home to bed.

This had been the first occasion that Wiggo had let me drive. The incident at Latchmere, although small, had I suppose proved that I had my wits about me when driving and the handling of the train I felt sure had left nothing to be desired. This now opened up a delightful chapter for me for, although I had been allowed to drive by my other drivers now and again, I discoverd over the next few days that this was now to become a regular thing, almost on a daily basis. On the following evening we booked on at 6.15 p.m. to work parts of three duties. The first was 473 duty; we prepared a Schools class (on the first day, 30911 *Dover*) and at 7.15 worked light engine to Victoria, where we got relieved by a Ramsgate crew, who worked the 7.35 to Ramsgate. We in turn then relieved on a light Pacific at 7.30. The duty as shown on the official sheet at the shed was shown as follows:—

	Arr.		Dep.	
10 Duty.		Victoria	7.40	Bank E.C.
	7.43	Eastern carriage sheds	7.50	E.C.
	7.53	Victoria	8.35	Bank/L.E.
	8.40	Stewarts Lane	9.00	E.C.
	9.10	Victoria	9.35	Bank/L.E.
	9.38	Eastern carriage sheds	10.15	Engine requirements/L.E.
	10.18	Victoria	To work 10.35 Ramsgate	

L.E. — Light Engine. E.C. — Empty coaching stock.
Relieved at 10.20 Relieve on 20 duty.

As will be seen, we then worked empty coaches into Victoria for the following two Ramsgate trains; this resulted in lengthy periods of inactivity standing in the platform. This could be interesting, however, in that sometimes conversations could be had with a passenger or two. Occasionally, we let spotters have a quick visit to the footplate. Now and then an old lady might come up and ask us if the train was stopping at such and such a place and, after assuring her it was, she warned us to be sure and stop there – even though our engine was at the wrong end of the train!

That was the terse official description of the shift, but perhaps translating it in more detail gives it a better flavour.

The engine had worked up a train from Ramsgate and at 7.40 we propelled this train of empty stock back into the sheds about a quarter of a mile south of the station. This was a fairly tricky operation where one had to have all one's wits at the ready. There was no engine at the leading end and, when the shunt signal cleared, he waved to the driver to propel back. The driver could not see the shunt signal but had to check the repeater was showing clear on the platform. We then propelled but, due to the passage over the points and a curve from the station up towards Grosvenor Bridge, we lost sight of the shunter, who was responsible for observing the signals en route as well as applying the brake from the guard's van if necessary. On the engine, the regulator had to be opened a fair bit to move the train up the grade quickly to avoid delay to the surburban train service, all the time carefully watching the train pipe gauge in case the brake was applied. Approaching the sheds, the pace had to be eased, to ensure one did not enter at too high a speed, to allow staff working there to get clear of the train, as well as to provide an opportunity for the shunter to take any action necessary should a wrong road have been set – with the possibility of a collision with an already occupied road. Reduction of speed could not be too great, however, or the engine and train could slip to a standstill on the last bit of severe up-grade into the sheds. This would result in the main line still being blocked. To help matters further, the curve into the shed was left-hand in the direction of travel and all the way from the station was a 10′ wall, so that until the whole train had entered the shed area, no-one on the footplate could see where the train was heading or any staff who might want to give hand signals to us. For emergency use, on the wall there was a large shunting bell operated from the sheds, which could be heard if one was within about ten feet of it; otherwise one just trusted in the good Lord.

Banking the engine away had its moments. All trains had to be given assistance out because of the fearsome Grosvenor bank up to the bridge of the same name across the Thames. It was the expected thing that the banking engine would be worked with full regulator and very little cut-off, to do the lion's share of the initial work and give a good start to the train engine. The only trouble about this was that one had to stop at a shunt signal after parting company with the train and on no account over-run it. This signal was only about three train lengths out of the station, so that one second the engine would be roaring in reverse at about 30 m.p.h. full regulator and nearly full gear, and then the regulator smartly shut, as the brake was fully applied. The last bit of this duty was in fact the most laborious for the fireman for, after banking away the 9.35 to Ramsgate, we ran light to Victoria carriage sheds, where there was a hand-turned turntable. Hand pushing a West Country Pacific on this was very hard work for both driver and fireman and we had to do this for the 10.35 Ramsgate.

After turning and moving off the table, the worst of the clinker had to be removed from the fire and then the usual huge Pacific fire built up. In this location, however, there were additional problems. Those who know the area will be aware that there is a very large block of flats bordering the shed. Making up the fire of any engine produces smoke, but Bulleid Pacifics could produce smoke like no other. The dense clouds were not welcomed by the flat residents, who protested in no uncertain terms. The only way to overcome this was to put on the blower. This in turn gave a problem, for the Pacifics concerned had the best-steaming boilers in the country and pressure even without the blower on could rise rapidly enough. Pressure would therefore rise towards the 280 pound mark and, when these engines blew off in what was virtually a concrete canyon, the amount of noise can be imagined.

A certain quantity of steam and water was used up in propelling the 9.35 and I put no water into the boiler until the safety valves gave an initial hiss of warning that they were about to lift in earnest. Then pressure would drop with the injector filling the boiler – but it was essential not to overfill to ensure that the engine did not prime when climbing Grosvenor bank. All in all, it was a delicate balancing act. After making the fire up, it was a case of pulling about a ton of coal forward in the tender and of filling the tender with water from the crane before backing down to the station – a busy end to this part of the turn. Next we went by electric train to Holborn Viaduct station and relieved on 20 duty. The engine was 31067 an E1 class 4-4-0 which had earlier worked in the only steam passenger train of the day to Holborn Viaduct. We then stayed on this train until the H class pilot shunted it off us and awaited the arrival at 12.30 a.m. of a van train which had come from Cannon Street. We worked this train tender-first via Loughborough Junction and Brixton to Victoria, arriving there at 1.00 a.m. This quarter of an hour's run, tender first in driving rain, could be a bit of a trial. On the first night I drove the engine on the last bit of the day's work, light back to the loco.

The following days were the same duties but it was clear that my mate's confidence in my driving was growing, for the next night he placed the West Country 34067 *Tangmere* in my charge from 9.10 onwards. This was the first time I had driven one of this class, except within the confines of the shed and I experienced quite a thrill in heaving open the regulator banking out the 9.35 – and managing to brake to stop short of the aforementioned shunt signal. The night after this I was given the E1 to drive throughout from relieving at Holborn to stowing at Stewarts Lane. The engine we had on this particular night was 31504. It was raining fairly hard when we left Holborn. I opened the long regulator and away we lunged tender-first towards Victoria. Perhaps I should have said leapt. There really was no other engine like them. They had been rebuilt with long-travel 10′ piston valves and they were indeed a driver's engine. Built to work Continental boat trains of ten or twelve coaches, they were very powerful and strong. They virtually gulped steam and had a very good front end, punching the exhaust to atmosphere, being very responsive to regulator and reverser. They were fast and, in addition, were also fairly lively engines; firing a rough one at speed could be a bit of a hit-and-miss affair. I pumped the steam reversing gear by feel to about 30 per cent cut-off and opened the main port of the regulator. It was exhilarating roaring through the dark, the engine shouting and throwing not a few sparks. Running at about 50 m.p.h. was not too much trouble as far as Loughborough Junction, as the signals were colour light and a quick glance into the cold stinging rain was all that was required. I shut the regulator to take the diverging junction to Brixton and cast an anxious look out for the first semaphore not far past the junction. Initially the tender obscured my view but, as soon as it appeared, I saw it was 'on'. Wiggo had also seen it from the fireman's side and shouted. A heavy application of the brakes was just in time, to bring us to a stand a couple of feet from the signal. After it had cleared, we ran nonstop until the shunter gave me a hand signal to stop, again a good application, and we came promptly and nicely to a halt.

Yes, very much a driver's engine but not so much a fireman's. They steamed well enough but those cylinders did gulp steam, which in turn used a fair bit of water. Many a time I found the demand over a distance exceeded the supply and it required driving taking advantage of road knowledge to make the task a reasonable one for the fireman. The following nights I was given charge of the Pacific from 9.15 and the 4-4-0 throughout. We had 31505 on the Wednesday, D1 31743 (there was no difference to the feel of them, they were the same as an E1) and 31504 again on the Friday.

The following week was an easy one as far as work, and times of work, were concerned. 58 duty required booking on at 7.35, preparing the engine, an L.M.S. type 2-6-4 tank, built at Brighton. All the week we had the same one, 42091. I can't recall the reason now but for some time this particular engine was not permitted to work passenger trains and at this period was limited to working locally. On this turn, after taking the usual train of empty stock to Victoria and banking them away (the 9.35 to Ramsgate), we ran light to Stewarts Lane for a Western Section train, for this was the Southern depot for the Pullman Car Company. The servicing and cleaning of the stock was undertaken there and it was worked daily to and from Clapham Junction. We worked them from the Lane at 11.05 to Clapham Junction, where an M7 backed onto the other end, and on to Waterloo for the 12.30 departure.

We then ran light to Eardley sidings on the Central section, where we took a leisurely time forming up and shunting coaching stock. This was mainly used on the Tunbridge Wells and associated Central Section services, as well as storing some of the extra coaching stock for the Eastern Section services. At a little after 3 o'clock, we trundled off to Stewarts Lane, disposed the engine and went home.

All the week I had done at least half the driving and I found that Wiggo liked a spell of firing. As I certainly enjoyed my part of the bargain, it seemed a fair exchange.

The following Monday, however, brought me back to normal with a bump, for Wiggo departed for a period of duty on the electrics. I was booked with Jack May to return for the day to my old stamping ground – Herne Hill Sorting sidings. Our engine was E2 No.32101, which I had last fired back in 1950, when it still sported the old pre-war Maunsell livery with the large numbers on the side tanks. Since then, she had been renumbered. It turned out that our reunion was not a happy one. As dawn broke, I removed the lamps from the rear of the bunker and, as I jumped to the ground, one of them slipped from my hand and landed fair and square on my right foot, with the result all further footplate activity ceased whilst I was off sick for a week.

On my return, Wiggo was still away and for a further week I did a different duty each day with a variety of engines, mostly short-distance turns with H class tanks or Moguls. On 27th October, however, he was back and we started work for a week on the Bellingham Goods. This particular duty illustrates how times have changed on railways. We booked on at 4.15 in the afternoon and ran empty to Island sidings at 4.30. These sidings were sandwiched between the viaduct carrying the main line from Victoria to the Kent coast, and the lines that ran from Stewarts Lane up a steep incline to join the main line at Wandsworth Road. We backed with our C class 0-6-0 onto the front of a rake of ten coaches. The damper was only slightly open, in order not to let the fire damp down too much, with the blower just on, to prevent smoke blowing back through the firedoors, which were open a few inches. We had to stand for about 15 minutes and care was taken that fuel was not wasted by the engine blowing off. On the other hand, we were going to start away with a heavy train on a 1 in 80 gradient, cross the junction onto the mainline and continue working up the same adverse gradient for about a mile until just beyond Clapham. And on the Southern we were paranoic when it came to timekeeping, for the suburban services were tightly timed and it was a real sin to delay them. We always used to follow the down Orpington electric, so as the time approached we looked for its appearance on the bridge passing over the loco. As soon as we saw it, I opened the damper fully, gave a turn on the blower and a splash of coal round the firebox. At the same time the driver opened the small ejector to start a slow release of the brakes, too quick a release meaning an application to stop the train rolling back before the signal was clear. At the right away, the safety valves should have just lifted with the full head of steam we now had; a short push of the large ejector to ensure the brakes were fully released and, with the gear in the full forward position, it was away, sand on and full regulator! The C class kept their feet fairly well and we gradually gained speed, although we were lucky to be exceeding 20 over the junction. With very little cut off, even in broad daylight a few bright sparks could be seen in the exhaust. As can be imagined, the noise of the C working so hard was impressive, the more so as there were rows of houses and brick walls in this part of London to throw the sound back; between blasts, sometimes, the echo could be heard on the footplate.

Once we were over the top at Clapham, lighter work was the order of the day, for most of the way was level or slightly down grade, running through Brixton, through Loughborough Junction and thence over the Thames and coasting into the old closed station of Ludgate Hill, with its island platform. The Thames bridge, built in 1868, over the last couple of years has been pulled down, for there are no empty stock working such as ours to pass over it since electrification; its other purpose was to carry to Ferme Park on Eastern Region or Cricklewood on the Midland, the then large numbers of cross-London transfer goods. In fact, after being uncoupled from our train at Ludgate Hill, we were about to descend into the tunnelled link between the North and South London railways, which these goods trains took. It was one of the strangest railway places in the country. We left Ludgate and passed a few hundred yards along the line under Holborn Viaduct station signal box, dropping down the 1 in 60 and into the tunnel beyond. Still descending rapidly, we plunged through the darkness until ahead was a shaft of light and another signal box placed in a corner of the tunnel wall itself, Snow Hill box – surely one of the worst places in the country to work in. It was on the site of the old Snow Hill station and was officially known as Holborn Low Level. However, it was generally referred to by its earlier name. Throughout the night and to a lesser extent during the off-peak periods of the day, heavy goods toiled up the steep incline, with a banking engine, usually an ex-G.N.R. N1 0-6-2 tank, blasting away at the rear. There was very little provision for steam and smoke to escape from the tunnel; all night, at the top end, smoke languorously issued forth. Now and again a train, even with the banker, would stall; when this happened, the engine of the next train would run forward light and be attached to the cavalcade which, with much slipping and belching forth sparks and clouds of black smoke, would gradually grind its way towards the surface again. In this convivial atmosphere dwelt the poor Snow Hill signalman! The banking turn was used as a punishment for Kings Cross drivers for minor misdemeanours but the Snow Hill signalman had to take it all as his normal day's or night's work!

At Snow Hill there was a junction. To the left (where we were bound) were the sidings, about ten in number, of Smithfield Market. This was a complete subterranean goods yard about the size of a football ground, situated under the market itself. To the right the junction continued on to join the widened lines of London Transport's Metropolitan Line at Farringdon. Meat trains from Western Region were worked from Paddington by condensing variants of the 5700 class tanks to the sidings where they were unloaded into cold stores. The sidings were ill lit and the whole area was in a permanent state of semi-darkness. Two kinds of wild life existed in this strange place – rats by the hundred and equally ferocious semi-wild cats, encouraged to keep the former occupants in check.

We arrived in the siding next to the through line, which was kept for light engine working, at about 5.30 and had about an hour and a quarter to wait before we moved. This was necessary to ensure that during the rush-hour period, only commuter trains were out and about – no goods trains or light engine working was allowed during this period.

As we had some time to kill, it was usual to make a can of tea and have a bite to eat; now and again on this turn I would wander down to the southern portal of the tunnel to have a look at the Metropolitan Line trains passing, full of homegoing breadwinners. At that time, apart from the red Uxbridge Line Metadyne stock trains, everything was virtually as the Metropolitan Railway had left it – the Aylesbury trains of teak steam stock hauled by Bo-Bo electric locomotives in war-time grey and the Watford trains, of T compartment stock. At long last, at about 6.45 p.m., the shunt signal at the top of the siding came off and we rushed headlong, light engine up the grade towards Holborn, and daylight again, Snow Hill and the tunnel disappearing behind us. Nine miles of non-stop light running ensued, turning onto the Catford loop line at Nunhead; this line, as well as being for suburban services, was a useful relief line from Victoria for Kent coast trains, joining the line from Victoria again at Shortlands, a mile north of Bromley South. We ran to Bellingham, and shunted back into the goods yard. The Catford area of London was served by this yard and, like dozens of others, its main purpose in life was the domestic coal traffic. Even in this one yard, there were three or four competing coal merchants, all taking a good number of wagons throughout the week. The only other trade was a builders' merchant, taking the odd wagon of bricks, slates or cement. Such was the traffic that we had about 45 minutes of shunting, knocking out the empties, replacing the loaded and making up our train to work forward to Bromley South. Having completed our shunting, at 8.45 we worked the train of empty wagons up the climb to Shortlands, then round the long swinging curve into Bromley South goods yard. Here we shunted more wagons from trains which had called earlier on in the day. On the down side there was a short branch which diverged down a slope next to the main line about half a mile south of the station and ended in the gas works. We delivered several wagon loads a day to this establishment and gathered the empties. After shunting the gas works, we took the empties over the main to the up side sidings. Here again there was a lot of traffic with the coal merchants, as well as a considerable builders' yard, whilst Bromley South had also a certain amount of bits-and-pieces traffic in the shape of furniture and general goods.

We worked engine-first out of London, so for the return journey it was tender-first. Of all types of locomotive work, tender-first was the most hated by footplate men. Firstly, of course, the tender obstructed the view ahead. This either meant leaning out of the side of the cab to look round the tender to observe the road and signals ahead or standing on tiptoe if the coal was at a low enough level, for the same purpose. There was a good chance of getting coal dust in the eyes despite efforts, prior to moving, to damp it down with the watering pipe. In addition, both for driving and firing, it was the wrong way. From the driver's point of view, it was a question of turning round to adjust cut-off, although operation of the regulator if mounted across the boiler, was no hardship. With a pull-out regulator, however, it was a matter of further contortions. For the fireman, keeping his feet was difficult when compared with normal running, the feel of the footplate being different; in addition, a number of classes of locomotives had damper arrangements which favoured forward running and made steam more difficult to get when running backwards.

On this first night, the driving had been handed over to me at Bellingham, and we had had a couple of good hours' shunting. Now we were to work the 11.10 p.m. goods from Bromley South to Herne Hill and we had 45 wagons on – quite a heavy load for a C class. The 'dummy' cleared, I knocked up the small ejector and in about five seconds the brakes were off. I opened the regulator on the first port and we moved gently backwards. Driving a loose-coupled goods is actually the most skilled type of driving there is as regards 'handling' a train. The start has to be gentle; if a 'snatch' is developed due to starting away too quickly, a loose coupling will go from hanging at rest to taut in a fraction of a second and breaks, the train then being in two parts. Instead the train has to be gradually eased away until all the couplings are stretched and when the whole train is on the move more power can then be applied. Care has also to be taken when reapplying power, particularly when one part of the train may be going uphill and the other down or again the train can break away.

The start from Bromley was downhill so, as soon as I felt the whole train on the move, I opened the regulator wide and we began to gather speed. I started bringing the cut-off back as we gathered momentum and passed through Shortlands then, leaving the Catford loop line on our right, we headed for Beckenham Junction. I could feel the weight of the 45 wagons now as, on full regulator and about 50 per cent cut-off, we climbed towards the 'bump' halfway between Shortlands and Beckenham. After passing over this and descending towards the station, I eased back to first port and brought the cut-off back. It was essential to get a good speed up here for we were near the start of the climb to the heights of Sydenham, below Crystal Palace. We bowled through Beckenham at about 40, the rumble of the train wheels clearly audible above the softened exhaust of the engine. Beckenham had a gantry at the London end of the station with three semaphore signals applicable to the line we were on; the tallest was off for us, indicating we were taking the through line to Victoria. Once clear of the points, I opened the regulator full, although I left the reverser at about 30 per cent. We gathered a bit more speed before the climb began up towards Kent House station. The grade gradually became stiffer and, as I felt a slight jerk on the engine telling me all couplings were tight throughout the train, I dropped the reverser back. The exhaust became a real staccato bark and the pyrotechnics began in earnest as small white hot pieces of coal shot skywards. Wiggo was firing little and often now in the time-honoured fashion, closing the firedoors between each shovelful. As we passed Kent House, we saw Penge distant was on; I gave a prolonged whistle, whereupon the home signal cleared. No doubt the starter was still on but we would still need all the power we had; any slackening now would mean a battle to get to the tunnel. Full back gear and doing about 15 m.p.h., we straightened in line with the station ahead and I saw the starting signal come off, telling us we were clear through the half a mile of Penge tunnel. When we entered, pressure was about 145 pounds, 15 below maximum, half a glass of water, and the exhaust at slow speed sounded throaty.

Penge tunnel was of yellow brick, with a blackened patch overhead. Looking over the low tender, without the boiler obstructing the view, it appeared to be a vast and endless cavern as we progressed, a cavern which echoed with the engine exhaust and the rumble of the train. We seemed an age getting to the middle, the grade only gradually levelling out. At this speed the tunnel was something to marvel at, particularly the fineness of the bricklaying, considering the millions of bricks involved. The engine had started to go downhill but there was no slackening in the working, for most of our train was still coming up the slope. Then gradually I was able to bring the reverser towards the mid position and just before we ran into the open , I shut the regulator. Almost immediately there was a jerk; the guard had applied his brake on the van. We passed through Sydenham Hill, gaining speed. The railway here is on a series of embankments of varying degree, and there is a gradual curve towards Herne Hill, some two miles from the exit of the tunnel. The train was doing about 30 m.p.h. and some way ahead of us was the outer home signal for Herne Hill station, with the distant below. The home was off but not the latter so I decided that I had better get hold of the train with a bit of brake. It was then I realised this was my first experience of a heavy goods train. The brake handle had a small pilot valve which, with a fitted train, was used to make a very light application; in the past with coaching stock I had used this to bring a slowly moving train to a stand. I proceeded to use the same technique with our present train and gave a light application. It was as though nothing had happened. I gave a moderate application with the brake handle; virtually no effect, in fact with a slight panic I thought we were going a bit faster. I gave a full application and this time the wagons ran on to us, their combined weight pushing hard against the engine.

I could hear the juddering of the tender brake gear as shocks were transmitted from it and looked apprehensively down the line, where Herne Hill seemed to be approaching at a lively pace. At last, however, we began to slow down perceptibly and, as we approached Herne Hill inner home, it fortunately cleared. I realised that I would have just about to come a stand short of it but this incident had been a salutary lesson to me, as it required all of half a mile to stop this train.

I released the brake, gave a slight touch of the regulator and we passed beneath the two boxes at Herne Hill into the Sorting sidings, grinding to a halt opposite the shunters' cabin. After unhooking, I drove the engine back to the Lane. And so to bed.

The following three nights followed the pattern of the first, except that we did not have such a heavy train on the last journey and on the Wednesday we had 31582. This C class was still lettered in Southern Railway style, with the legend BRITISH RAILWAYS in full on the tender instead of the usual emblem.

The next week we had the departmental shunting turn which I have mentioned before, with C and E2 class engines. Then on the following week we did 46 duty; this was a turn which took us mostly into areas that were normally the province of Bricklayers Arms shed. It was interesting from that point of view. This turn booked on a little earlier than the Bellingham Goods duty but started in much the same manner. It was an H class tank turn and at 4.15 was light engine to Island sidings, working the 4.30 empty stock train to Ludgate. After running round this train, we worked it via Blackfriars into Cannon Street and it became there the 5.45 Kent Coast departure.

After the latter left, we coupled to another H class tank and ran light to the sidings at Rotherhithe Road, near Bricklayers Arms. We worked vans from there to London Bridge (Low level) the former Brighton side of London Bridge and, after a bit of shunting, we pulled the night mail train into the platform, there steam heating it until we were relieved at 10.45. Then home by the South London line. On the 15th November 1952, I worked on Battle of Britain 34069 *Hawkinge* and found that her boiler pressure had been reduced from 280 to 250 pounds per square inch. This was one of the first of the class to be so modified; in the fullness of time all were similarly dealt with.

It is a truism that all good things come to an end, and a fortnight later I worked with Wiggo as my rostered mate for the last time, with C class 31583. I was being promoted to the Brighton main line goods link. It had been fun while it lasted. . . .